Order in the Chaos

Order in the Chaos

How to Think Clearly in a Noisy World

Andrea Hoxie

Published by Grand Pea Inc.
United States of America

ISBN: 979-8-9949284-0-0

Contents

A few months ago, while packing to move back into my childhood home, I came across boxes of supplements, devices, powders, capsules, and "healthy" drink mixes. Each one had promised improvement. Each one carried a monthly cost — often $40 or $70 — and I frequently purchased several months at a time. As I looked at those containers, I calculated what that money could have done elsewhere. Conserved and redirected, it could have provided meaningful support for a family for months. That realization was not about guilt. It was about discipline. It was clarifying.

From that point forward, I resolved to scrutinize what I read and examine what I hear. I resolved to pause before responding to urgency, scarcity, or emotional pressure. I resolved to apply the same diligence to my own decisions that I advise for others. This book is not about fear. It is not about cynicism. It is about discernment.

Throughout my career, I have seen the cost of poor planning, misunderstood policies, inflated promises, and unchecked assumptions. I have also seen the stability that comes when individuals take time to understand their options and act with intention.

Whether your goal is physical health, financial security, or spiritual grounding, wise decisions require clarity. And clarity requires discipline.

If this guide accomplishes anything, I hope it helps you slow down, think clearly, and prepare responsibly — not because of fear, but because order nurtures peace.

Let us begin.

Introduction:

Why This Book Exists in 2026

We are living in a time of extraordinary access to information — and extraordinary confusion. Never before have so many voices been able to reach us instantly. With a handheld device, we can access financial advice, medical opinions, political commentary, investment opportunities, and health guidance in seconds. On its face, this is remarkable. Yet information without discernment does not produce wisdom. It produces noise.

Since 1999, I have worked in insurance and financial advisory services, helping individuals, families, and small businesses navigate Medicare, health insurance, Social Security strategy, long-term care planning, and related regulatory systems. Over those decades, I have witnessed both the benefits of sound preparation and the lasting consequences of rushed or poorly informed decisions.

In recent years, I have observed a troubling acceleration. The speed of communication has increased, but the discipline of evaluation has weakened. Advertisements resemble journalism. Opinion is packaged as fact. Urgency replaces reflection. The line between professional guidance and persuasive marketing has become increasingly blurred. This shift affects more than purchasing decisions. It affects health outcomes. Retirement security. Estate planning. Family stability. Even trust itself.

Most financial or healthcare crises are not caused by catastrophe alone. They are often compounded by misunderstanding, delay, misplaced trust, or incomplete information. A supplement purchased in haste. An investment accepted without due diligence.

A policy canceled before replacement is secured. A benefit claimed without understanding its long-term implications.

At the same time, cultural pressures reward immediacy. We are urged to "act now," to "secure the limited supply," to "unlock the hidden solution." Simplicity is sold in a world that has become structurally complex.

Integrity still exists. There are honorable professionals in every field. There are ethical businesses and responsible institutions. But alongside them are opportunists who understand how to exploit uncertainty — particularly among seniors and those navigating health or financial vulnerability.

In 2026, the stakes are higher than they were a decade ago. Healthcare systems are consolidating. Digital privacy is increasingly fragile. Investment offerings are marketed with polished sophistication. Social media platforms amplify persuasive narratives without requiring proof.

Preparation is no longer optional. It is a responsibility. This resource guide was created to provide something steady in the midst of acceleration. It does not promise shortcuts. It does not offer miracle cures. It does not attempt to replace individualized professional advice. Instead, it aims to equip readers with foundational clarity — the kind that supports sound decisions over time.

Order nurtures peace. Peace produces stability. Stability protects families.

If you approach the following pages with patience and reflection, you will not find instant answers. You will find frameworks. Questions to ask. Red flags to notice. Disciplined approaches to evaluating claims. Practical tools to strengthen your decision-making.

That is enough. May this guide serve you well.

Part I

Health & Medical Reality

Chapter 1

Long Term Care: Planning Before the Crisis

The Policy I Let Go

In 1996, I was diagnosed with pulmonary sarcoidosis. A few years later, after my condition stabilized, I qualified for and purchased a long-term care insurance policy ("LTC"). The premiums were manageable. I paid them faithfully; I understood the value of the coverage.

In 2009, during a medical relapse and a significant change in my living situation, I experienced a period of financial strain. Under pressure, I made a decision that many people make: I allowed the long-term care policy to lapse.

At the time, my reasoning felt practical. I believed that the accumulated cash value would be returned to me and that I could re-enter the market later if necessary.

That is not what happened. The insurer applied the accumulated value to keep the policy in force until those funds were exhausted. By the time the coverage formally terminated, the safety net was gone.

A few years later, when my finances had stabilized, I attempted to purchase comparable long-term care coverage again. The premium was now about four and a half times what I had originally paid. Age had increased. Health history had evolved. The underwriting environment had tightened. Eventually, I could no longer qualify at all. What felt like short-term financial relief in 2009 became a permanent long-term consequence.

Statistics consistently show that most individuals will require some form of long-term care during their lifetime. I knew this professionally. I advise clients accordingly. Yet under financial pressure, I made the same mistake many families make — prioritizing the immediate strain over the future probability. That lesson has never left me.

When I began working in insurance in 1999, the first company I contracted with specialized in long-term care insurance. I remember suggesting that we market policies more aggressively to younger individuals. My reasoning was simple: the premiums would be lower, and long-term care is not exclusively an "old age" issue.

The idea was not warmly received. Commissions, after all, are driven by premium size. But I continued to encourage younger clients to consider coverage. I would often say: "If you forego one discretionary expense each week, you could significantly protect your future." It was practical advice. It remains practical advice.

More recently, on December 28, 2025, I experienced a series of falls — four in total, and one near-fall that I was fortunate to correct before impact. Each incident carried the same quiet question: What if something had broken?

I do not currently hold a traditional long-term care policy. I have an alternative arrangement with limited benefits. It is better than nothing. But I am acutely aware of its limitations. And that awareness shapes my decisions daily.

In my practice, I regularly receive urgent calls: "What can we do? Mom needs care now." "Is there a policy we can buy today?" "How do we qualify for Medicaid quickly?" When care is needed immediately, the options are limited, expensive, and stressful. Planning is most effective before crisis — not during it.

My experience is not unique. It is instructive. Long-term care planning is not about fear. It is about probability. It is about preserving dignity, protecting family members from preventable burden, and creating options while options still exist. The earlier the planning begins, the more flexible and affordable the solutions. The longer the delay, the narrower the path becomes.

National Long-Term Care Cost Snapshot (Median Estimates based on recent national median cost surveys such as Genworth Cost of Care reports. Costs vary by region and level of care.)

Type of Care	National Median Monthly Cost	National Median Annual Cost
Home Health Aide (44 hrs/week)	~$5,700	~$68,000
Assisted Living Facility	~$4,800	~$57,600
Nursing Home (Semi-Private Room)	~$8,900	~$106,800
Nursing Home (Private Room)	~$10,000	~$120,000

Important: Many metropolitan areas exceed these amounts significantly. Inflation in long-term care services has historically outpaced general inflation.

The Long-Term Care Decision Ladder

Planning is not one-size-fits-all. Options vary based on health, age, assets, and risk tolerance.

Step 1 – Self-Insure

Sufficient liquid assets to cover $100,000+ annually for multiple years

Clear estate plan

Family alignment

Willingness to spend down assets

Risk: Rapid asset depletion if extended care is required.

Step 2 – Traditional Long-Term Care Insurance

Stand-alone policy

Lower initial premiums (younger purchase age)

Inflation rider critical

Subject to premium increases over time

Risk: Premium increases; underwriting qualification required.

Step 3 – Hybrid/Asset-Based LTC

Life insurance or annuity with LTC rider

Typically guaranteed premium

Death benefit if care not used

Higher initial commitment

Risk: Larger upfront cost; still requires underwriting.

Step 4 – Limited Alternative Arrangements

Short-term care policies

Indemnity-style coverage

Health-sharing or niche products

Risk: Benefit caps; coverage gaps.

Step 5 – Medicaid Planning (Last Resort Strategy)

Strict income and asset rules

Five-year lookback period

Limited facility choice in some cases

Risk: Reduced flexibility and asset protection if planning not done early.

When You Cannot Qualify for Coverage
If underwriting disqualifies you:

Explore hybrid options if health permits.
Evaluate partial self-insurance with earmarked funds.
Review Medicaid eligibility rules before crisis.
Consider home modification and fall prevention investments.
Engage in realistic family planning discussions.

The key is this: once you are uninsurable, your options narrow dramatically.

Key Takeaways

Long-term care is a probability, not a remote possibility.

Costs nationally exceed $100,000 per year for skilled nursing care.

Premiums increase significantly with age and health changes.

A lapse decision can have permanent consequences.

Planning before crisis preserves dignity and options.

The earlier the planning begins, the more affordable and flexible the solutions.

What You Should Do Next –

☐ Determine whether you currently have long-term care coverage.

☐ Review policy benefits, inflation riders, and elimination periods.

☐ If uninsured, request an illustration while you are still insurable.

☐ Discuss realistic family expectations — do not assume children can absorb full-time care.

☐ Evaluate whether your assets can withstand 2–4 years of care expenses.

☐ Revisit your estate and beneficiary designations.

☐ Do not wait for a diagnosis or a fall to begin the conversation.

Key Takeaways
Traditional and hybrid policies solve different problems.
Younger purchase age increases affordability.
Inflation protection is critical.
Waiting narrows options.
Underwriting becomes more restrictive over time.

What You Should Do Next
- ☐ Determine which category fits your asset profile.
- ☐ Request illustrations for both structures (if insurable).
- ☐ Compare total projected lifetime cost — not just first-year premium.
- ☐ Evaluate inflation rider impact.
- ☐ Confirm carrier financial strength ratings.

Professional Disclaimer: Policy features, premium structures, and rider availability vary by carrier and state. Underwriting approval is required. Readers should review policy contracts carefully and consult licensed professionals before purchasing coverage.

Chapter 3

Medicare Basics That People Get Wrong

Clarifying Coverage Before It Becomes Expensive

Medicare confusion is one of the most common and costly misunderstandings I encounter. Many assume:

Medicare is "free."

Medicare covers long-term care.

Medicare Advantage and Medicare Supplement are interchangeable.

You can hold multiple supplements.

Enrollment timing does not matter.

Each assumption can lead to avoidable financial consequences.

What Medicare Does NOT Cover – Medicare does not pay for:

Custodial long-term care

Extended assisted living stays

Ongoing nursing home residency beyond limited skilled benefit periods

This misunderstanding alone causes major planning failures.

Enrollment Timing Rules

Key periods:

Initial Enrollment Period (IEP)

Special Enrollment Period (SEP)

Open Enrollment Period (OEP)

Late enrollment can result in:
Permanent premium penalties
Coverage gaps
Underwriting requirements

Medicare Supplement vs. Medicare Advantage

Feature	Medicare Supplement (Medigap)	Medicare Advantage
Network	Nationwide	HMO/PPO networks
Referrals	Not required	Often required
Predictability	High	Variable cost sharing
Underwriting	Required after open enrollment	Generally not
Out-of-Pocket Maximum	No cap under original Medicare; supplement bridges the gap in coverage	Required annual cap

Neither is universally "better." Suitability depends on health status, risk tolerance, travel, and financial predictability preference.

Duplicate Medicare Supplement Coverage -- Federal law prohibits holding more than one Medicare Supplement policy simultaneously. If applying for a new supplement:

Do not cancel existing coverage until new coverage is approved.
Coordinate effective dates carefully.
Document submission timelines.

Administrative delays can create exposure if not handled properly.

Extra Help (Low-Income Subsidy) -- Qualification is based on:

Income
Resources
Marital status

Incarceration, spousal status, and living arrangements can complicate eligibility analysis. Misreporting can trigger overpayment recovery.

Key Takeaways

Medicare does not equal long-term care coverage.
Enrollment timing matters.
Supplements and Advantage plans function differently.
Duplicate supplement policies are prohibited.
Administrative precision prevents financial loss.

What You Should Do Next

Review your current Medicare structure.
Confirm enrollment period status.
Verify that no duplicate supplement exists.
Confirm drug coverage adequacy annually.
Reassess coverage after major health changes.

Professional Disclaimer: Medicare rules and plan availability vary by state and year. This material is educational only and not a substitute for individualized plan analysis.

Chapter 4

Vertical Integration in Healthcare

Vertical integration is the hidden architecture behind many of the frustrations people feel in health care but can't quite name. Here is my "plain English" discussion.

Vertical integration occurs when one corporate family controls multiple levels of the health-care supply chain, instead of independent entities competing with one another. In health care, this often means one parent company owns:

A health insurance company
A Pharmacy Benefit Manager (PBM)
Pharmacies (retail, mail-order, specialty)
Physician practices
Clinics or urgent care centers
Data and analytics platforms

What used to be checks and balances has become one continuous pipeline.

Real-World Examples (No Speculation)

UnitedHealth Group
Insurer: UnitedHealthcare
PBM: OptumRx
Providers: Optum Health (physicians, clinics)
Data & analytics: Optum Insight

CVS Health
Insurer: Aetna
PBM: CVS Caremark
Pharmacies: CVS retail, mail-order, specialty
Clinics: MinuteClinic

Cigna Group
Insurer: Cigna
PBM: Express Scripts

This is not accidental consolidation. It is deliberate strategy.

The Claimed Benefits (The Sales Pitch)

1. "Better Coordination of Care" -- In theory:
   Fewer silos
   Shared data
   Streamlined decision-making

This can help some patients with well-managed chronic care when incentives align.

2. "Lower Costs Through Efficiency" -- In theory:
   Fewer middlemen
   Less duplication
   Administrative savings

Again, possible— but not guaranteed.

3. "Convenience for Patients" -- One ecosystem:
   Same card
   Same app
   Same pharmacy
   Same clinic

Convenience is real — but convenience is not the same as choice.

The Real Risks (Where the Trouble Starts)

1. Conflicts of Interest Become Structural -- When the same entity:

Decides what drugs are covered
Sets reimbursement rates
Owns the pharmacy
Employs the doctor

Financial incentives quietly replace independent judgment. No single decision looks outrageous — but the cumulative effect is powerful.

2. Steering, Not Choice -- Patients may be:

Nudged toward "preferred" pharmacies
Penalized for using independent providers
Forced into mail-order or specialty pharmacies owned by the PBM

This is economic steering, not free-market competition.

3. Independent Providers Get Squeezed Out -- Independent:

Pharmacies
Physician practices
Community clinics

often face:

Lower reimbursement
Delayed payments
Take-it-or-leave-it contracts

Result: closures, deserts of care, and loss of personalized service.

4. Data Power Concentration -- Integrated entities hold:

Medical claims
Pharmacy claims
Behavioral data
Utilization patterns

That data shapes:

Coverage decisions
Pricing strategies
Network inclusion

Patients rarely know how their data is used or leveraged.

5. Accountability Gets Murky -- When something goes wrong:

Insurer blames PBM
PBM blames formulary rules
Provider blames prior authorization
Pharmacy blames reimbursement contracts

But they're all under one corporate roof.

Why Seniors Are Especially Affected -- For older adults:

Medicare Advantage plans are often highly integrated
Drug formularies, provider networks, and pharmacies are tightly linked
Switching plans or providers mid-year is difficult or impossible

Vertical integration can quietly:

Lock seniors into narrow ecosystems
Limit access to trusted doctors or pharmacies
Increase out-of-pocket drug costs
Reduce real choice — while appearing seamless

The Big Truth

Vertical integration can improve efficiency but without strong guardrails, it also:

Weakens competition
Blurs fiduciary responsibility
Concentrates power
Shifts decision-making away from patients

This is why regulators, states, and Congress are increasingly scrutinizing it — though oversight has lagged behind consolidation.

Bottom Line for Clients

When one company controls the insurance, the drug benefit, the pharmacy, and the provider, the system may work smoothly — but not always in the patient's favor. Understanding this structure helps explain:

Why appeals are harder

Why options are narrower

Why "convenient" isn't always "best"

Chapter 5

Supplements: Evidence vs. Hype

How to Spot Health Hype -- A quick guide for discerning consumers

• Fear first, facts later" Urgent language ("act now," "hidden danger," "doctors won't tell you") is a tell. Credible health guidance informs; it doesn't alarm.

• Real science, distorted meaning: Scientific terms are often used correctly — then stretched beyond evidence. Words like toxins, inflammation, buildup, and detox deserve careful scrutiny.

• One cause blamed for many conditions: High blood pressure, fatigue, pain, and memory changes rarely share a single cause. Be wary of one-size-fits-all explanations.

• Diagnosis and cure sold together: If the same source identifies the problem and sells the solution, slow down. Independent verification matters.

• Conventional care quietly dismissed: Responsible health information doesn't pit natural approaches against medical science — it integrates them appropriately.

• Testimonials over data: Personal stories can be encouraging but aren't proof. Look for well-designed human studies, not just before-and-after claims.

• Vague promises, no specifics: Phrases like "supports detox" or "cleanses the kidneys" sound impressive but often lack measurable meaning.

Rule of thumb: If a health claim makes a complex issue sound simple, urgent, and secretly fixable — pause.

A good chunk of "adulting" calls for wisdom, discernment, and measured judgment. In matters of health, discernment means resisting fear, asking good questions, and honoring both truth and the body entrusted to our care. Health hype often thrives on anxiety — yet fear is a poor guide for decision-making. Discernment asks:

Is this claim balanced, or is it exaggerated?
Does it invite understanding, or demand urgency?
Does it respect knowledge built over time, or dismiss it entirely?

Stewardship of health is not about chasing every new claim, but about thoughtful care — informed by evidence, experience, and sound counsel. Wisdom is rarely loud, rushed, or secret.

Questions to Ask Your Doctor: Before acting on a health claim, ask:

1. Is this concern supported by solid evidence in people like me?
2. Is this exposure or condition common enough to explain my symptoms?
3. What tests, if any, would be appropriate — and why?
4. Could this interfere with my current medications or conditions?
5. What proven steps should come first before experimental ones?
6. Is there any harm in waiting, monitoring, or doing nothing right now?

Reminder: Good clinicians welcome thoughtful questions. Shared decision-making is a strength, not a challenge.

Beetroot & Blood Pressure

How It Works — The Mechanism **--** Beet juice may help lower blood pressure because it contains nitrates. The body converts nitrates to nitric oxide, a compound that helps relax and widen blood vessels. Beyond nitrates, beetroot also contains other active compounds — including betalains, flavonoids, polyphenols, saponins, and vitamin C — all of which contribute to vasodilation.

What the Research Shows -- Systolic & Diastolic Reduction **--** Across 22 randomized clinical trials, systolic blood pressure was significantly lower in beetroot juice-supplemented groups (by approximately 3.55 mmHg) and diastolic blood pressure by approximately 1.32 mmHg, compared to control groups.

Dosage & Duration

• Drinking about 250 mL of beet juice daily appears to produce the best outcomes for lowering blood pressure.

• Noticeable effects can begin within a few hours, with sustained benefits observed after 60 days.

• The effect on systolic blood pressure is larger with longer study durations (14 days or more) and with higher doses — a positive correlation exists between dosage and degree of blood pressure reduction.

Hypertensive Patients Specifically -- 2024 meta-analysis (Nutrition, Metabolism & Cardiovascular Diseases) found that beetroot juice lowers clinical systolic blood pressure in hypertensive patients, with a significant effect observed up to 90 days of intervention. However, evidence does not support a prolonged 24-hour blood pressure reduction.

Important Nuances & Limitations -- Oral Health Matters -- A 2025 study (npj Biofilms and Microbiomes) found that the blood pressure-lowering effect of beetroot juice is impaired in patients with periodontitis, but recovers after periodontal treatment. In healthy individuals, both systolic and diastolic blood pressure decreased significantly 90 minutes after beetroot juice intake — but not in periodontitis patients. Key Reason: Nitrate must be converted by bacteria in the mouth before the body can use it. Gum disease disrupts this conversion process, reducing or eliminating the blood pressure benefit.

Older Adults with Treated Hypertension -- A 2024 randomized placebo-controlled study (RSC Food & Function) of adults aged 56-71 with treated hypertension found that increased nitrate intake from beetroot juice over 4 weeks did not sustainably improve vascular function or lower blood pressure in this population group. This suggests results may vary significantly depending on age and existing medication regimens.

Not a Replacement for Medication -- While beetroot juice can help lower blood pressure, it may not be as effective as medications prescribed for high blood pressure. Patients should always discuss any complementary approach with their physician before making changes to their treatment plan.

Key Takeaways for Community Education

• Beetroot juice is a promising adjunct to — not a substitute for — prescribed blood pressure management.Complementary, not replacement:

• 250 mL daily appears most effective based on current meta-analyses.Optimal dose:

• Effects begin within a few hours; benefits can sustain 60-90 days with consistent use.Onset and duration:

• Good oral/dental health is required for the nitrate-to-nitric oxide conversion to work properly. Patients with gum disease may see reduced benefit.Dental health connection:

• Results are less consistent in older adults already on blood pressure medications — manage expectations accordingly.Variability in older adults:

• Always advise clients and community members to consult their physician before adding beetroot juice to their regimen.Professional guidance:

Note for Insurance & Advocacy Context: Understanding natural interventions like beetroot juice helps clients make informed decisions about their overall health management — which can affect health insurance outcomes, medication adherence, and long-term wellness planning.

CoQ10 & Statin Conversations

What CoQ10 Is **--** Coenzyme Q10 (CoQ10), also known as ubiquinone, is a compound naturally produced in the body that plays a central role in energy production within the cell's mitochondria. It also functions as an antioxidant, protecting cells from oxidative damage.

Why Statins Deplete CoQ10 -- Statins lower CoQ10 levels because they share a biochemical manufacturing process. Statins work by inhibiting the enzyme HMG-CoA reductase — the rate-limiting step in the mevalonate pathway responsible for synthesizing cholesterol. This same mevalonate pathway also produces CoQ10, which explains why statin use leads to reduced concentrations of CoQ10 in the bloodstream. A 2024 study of statin-naive heart attack patients found that initiating statin treatment significantly decreased plasma CoQ10 levels by 43% over just three months. (MDPI International Journal of Molecular Sciences, December 2024)

Statin-Associated Muscle Symptoms (SAMS) -- Statins are among the most widely prescribed drugs for treating high cholesterol and reducing the risk of heart disease and stroke. However, they come with a wide range of side effects including myopathy, necrotizing rhabdomyolysis, diabetes, hepatotoxicity, and sleep problems. The most common side effect is statin-induced myopathy, which often leads to discontinuation of statin therapy and patient noncompliance.

When mitochondria malfunction from CoQ10 depletion, it can lead to skeletal muscle atrophy, generation of reactive oxygen species, impaired mitochondrial function, and programmed cell death — resulting in complaints ranging from mild muscle pain to rhabdomyolysis (a serious breakdown of muscle tissue).

What the Research Shows on CoQ10 Supplementation

Positive Findings

- A meta-analysis published in the Journal of the American Heart Association found that CoQ10 supplementation significantly reduced statin-associated muscle symptoms including muscle pain, muscle weakness, muscle cramps, and muscle tiredness — compared to placebo.
- A 2024 systematic review of 800 patients (Cureus) found that all randomized controlled trials showed improvement in statin-associated myopathy with CoQ10 supplementation, with or without a reduced statin dosage, and with no notable side effects from CoQ10 itself.
- A 2025 meta-analysis (PMC/Justus Liebig University) found an overall significant reduction in muscle pain (measured by pain intensity scores) after CoQ10 supplementation in statin-treated patients, with dosages ranging from 100 to 600 mg per day over 30 to 90 days.

Mixed and Cautionary Findings

- A 2025 review noted that while CoQ10 led to modest symptom reduction in some patients, overall evidence remains inconclusive and is not sufficiently robust to justify universal supplementation. Neither the American Heart Association nor the FDA officially recommends CoQ10 for all statin users.
- One randomized, double-blinded, placebo-controlled trial found that CoQ10 supplementation had no measurable effect on muscle CoQ10 levels or mitochondrial function and did not affect

myalgia symptoms — highlighting that results across studies are not uniform.

Bottom line: Research is promising but divided. CoQ10 may be especially worth considering for patients experiencing persistent muscle symptoms who are at risk of stopping their statin therapy — a clinical decision that always belongs to the treating physician.

Dosage & How to Take It

- 100 mg to 200 mg daily; some clinical trials used up to 600 mg.Typical studied dose:
- CoQ10 is fat-soluble. It should be taken with a meal containing dietary fat to maximize absorption.Take with fat:
- Two forms available:
- Ubiquinone (oxidized form) — the standard, less expensive form
- Ubiquinol (reduced, active form) — often marketed as better absorbed, particularly for older adults whose conversion ability may be diminished

Drug Interactions to Know

- CoQ10 may reduce warfarin's (a blood thinner) effectiveness and increase the risk of blood clotting; it requires monitoring.
- CoQ10 has a blood pressure-lowering effect. Combining with blood pressure drugs could cause pressure to drop too low.
- CoQ10 may help regulate blood sugar and improve insulin sensitivity — creating a potential additive effect that requires careful blood glucose monitoring.

Key Takeaways for Community Education

- Statins deplete CoQ10 — this is a documented biological fact, not a theory.
- Muscle pain is the most common reason patients stop taking statins — a serious compliance problem with life-or-death implications for cardiovascular patients.

- CoQ10 supplementation may help reduce muscle symptoms but evidence is mixed — it is not a guaranteed or universal solution.
- 100–200 mg daily with a fatty meal is the standard studied dose; ubiquinol may absorb better in older adults.
- CoQ10 is generally considered safe with no notable adverse effects at standard doses.
- Always advise consulting the prescribing physician — especially for patients on warfarin, blood pressure medications, or diabetes drugs.

Note for Insurance & Advocacy Context: Statin noncompliance due to muscle side effects is a major driver of cardiovascular events and hospitalizations. Educating clients about CoQ10 as a potential complementary option — paired with physician guidance — supports medication adherence and long-term health outcomes.

Functional Mushrooms

Functional mushrooms refer to nutrient-rich mushroom types used in functional medicine — they are not psychedelic. They are distinguished by their adaptogenic properties that offer support beyond basic nutritional value, including immune system health, stress response, and brain health. They exhibit a broad spectrum of pharmacological activity and have been used for thousands of years as both food and medicine in traditional Chinese and Eastern medicine.

The most studied varieties are:

- Lion's Mane (Hericium erinaceus) — brain, nerve, cognitive function
- Reishi (Ganoderma lucidum) — immune support, stress, sleep, known as the "mushroom of immortality"
- Chaga (Inonotus obliquus) — antioxidants, immunity, inflammation
- Cordyceps — energy, stamina, athletic performance
- Turkey Tail — gut health, immunity, cancer support research

The Pros

1. Immune Support -- Functional mushrooms contain beta-glucans, terpenes, and fungal immunomodulatory proteins that modulate the immune system by stimulating immune response genes. They have demonstrated anti-inflammatory, antioxidant, and antitumor properties in research settings.

2. Brain & Cognitive Function -- Studies have shown that Lion's Mane extract may help improve cognitive performance, overall mood, and reduce stress. It has also been studied for its role in nerve regeneration, with potential cognitive benefits particularly for older adults.

3. Stress Response & Adaptogenic Effects -- Adaptogens increase the body's resistance to physical, biological, and chemical stress, help promote healthy functioning during times of stress, and protect against stress-related damage. Research studies have shown that Lion's Mane, Cordyceps, and Reishi generally have good safety and tolerability when taken in supplement form.

4. Energy & Athletic Performance-- Cordyceps supports energy and stamina and is particularly noted for athletes or anyone seeking a natural boost for workouts or sustained activity during long days.

5. Gut Health -- The more established benefits surrounding mushrooms are tied to their richness in prebiotic fibers, which keep the microbiome healthy by giving beneficial microbes the food they need to stay alive. Note: eating the whole mushroom is the only way to obtain these prebiotic fibers — supplements may not provide this benefit.

6. Cancer Supportive Care -- Reishi contains approximately 400 different bioactive compounds, among which triterpenoids and polysaccharides are the two major active anti-cancer constituents. Triterpenoids are recognized for anti-inflammatory and antitumor activities, while polysaccharides activate macrophages and natural

killer cells, supporting immune surveillance and tumor elimination. Reishi is increasingly used for symptom control by cancer patients. (Memorial Sloan Kettering Cancer Center / PMC, 2024)

7. Growing Market & Scientific Validation -- The global functional mushroom market was valued at approximately $31.71 billion in 2023 and is projected to reach $65.83 billion by 2030 — a compound annual growth rate of 11.2%, significantly outpacing many traditional supplement categories. Consumer adoption has reached 37% of surveyed consumers reporting consumption of mushroom-enhanced foods and beverages.

> *Historical note: Reishi has been used in traditional Chinese medicine since at least 206 BC. It is now listed in the American Herbal Pharmacopoeia, the Chinese Pharmacopoeia, and the Therapeutic Compendium, and is widely used as an adjuvant in the treatment of various cancers.*

The Cons

1. Most Research Still Preliminary -- While some of the claimed benefits of functional mushrooms have research support, most of the research has been conducted in animal models. More robust human clinical trials are needed before definitive conclusions can be drawn. Observational studies often have limitations and do not offer conclusive evidence.

2. No FDA Oversight of Health Claims -- While producers must follow FDA guidelines to ensure product safety, the FDA does not test or validate the purported health claims of functional mushroom products. Consumers must exercise their own due diligence.

3. Lack of Industry Standardization -- The current lack of standardization and regulation in the functional mushroom industry means that product quality and potency vary widely. Without clear

guidelines, verifying the consistency and accuracy of health claims is difficult. Just because a product is natural does not automatically mean it is effective or safe.

4. Supplement Form vs. Whole Food -- Eating the whole mushroom is the only way to obtain prebiotic fibers — the most established nutritional benefit. Processed supplements may not deliver the same value as whole food consumption. Consumers should not assume that a capsule or powder is equivalent to the whole food.

5. Drug Interactions & Contraindications -- Before trying functional mushrooms, it is important to consult a healthcare professional, as they may cause side effects or interact with medications. Key interaction risks include:

- Blood thinners (e.g., warfarin): Reishi may enhance anticoagulant effects
- Immunosuppressive medications: mushrooms' immune-stimulating properties may counteract these drugs
- Diabetes medications: some mushrooms may lower blood sugar, creating additive effects
- Blood pressure medications: potential for additive blood pressure-lowering effects

6. Allergic Reactions & Contamination Risk -- The main safety risk comes from allergic reactions or product contamination. Functional mushrooms have a short shelf life of one to three days due to high water content, making post-harvest transportation and storage critical. Quality control in the supply chain — particularly from international sources — is an ongoing concern.

Caution: Some functional mushroom products on the market combine multiple mushroom species with other herbs and supplements. These combination products carry additional interaction risks that are not always well-studied.

Smart Consumer Guidance

- Look for third-party tested supplements bearing the USP or NSF certification seal.
- Consult NatMed.com or speak with a pharmacist to check for drug-supplement interactions.
- When possible, consume whole mushrooms (cooked) rather than relying solely on supplements.
- Always consult a physician or registered dietitian before adding functional mushrooms to a health regimen — especially for anyone managing chronic conditions, taking prescription medications, or undergoing cancer treatment.
- Be skeptical of products making extravagant health claims without published human clinical trial data to back them up.

Hydrogen Water & Trend Claims

Functional mushrooms refer to nutrient-rich mushroom types used in functional medicine — they are not psychedelic. They are distinguished by their adaptogenic properties that offer support beyond basic nutritional value, including immune system health, stress response, and brain health. They exhibit a broad spectrum of pharmacological activity and have been used for thousands of years as both food and medicine in traditional Chinese and Eastern medicine.

The most studied varieties are:

- Lion's Mane (Hericium erinaceus) — brain, nerve, cognitive function
- Reishi (Ganoderma lucidum) — immune support, stress, sleep, known as the "mushroom of immortality"
- Chaga (Inonotus obliquus) — antioxidants, immunity, inflammation
- Cordyceps — energy, stamina, athletic performance
- Turkey Tail — gut health, immunity, cancer support research

The Pros

1. Immune Support -- Functional mushrooms contain beta-glucans, terpenes, and fungal immunomodulatory proteins that modulate the immune system by stimulating immune response genes. They have demonstrated anti-inflammatory, antioxidant, and antitumor properties in research settings.

2. Brain & Cognitive Function -- Studies have shown that Lion's Mane extract may help improve cognitive performance, overall mood, and reduce stress. It has also been studied for its role in nerve regeneration, with potential cognitive benefits particularly for older adults.

3. Stress Response & Adaptogenic Effects -- Adaptogens increase the body's resistance to physical, biological, and chemical stress, help promote healthy functioning during times of stress, and protect against stress-related damage. Research studies have shown that Lion's Mane, Cordyceps, and Reishi generally have good safety and tolerability when taken in supplement form.

4. Energy & Athletic Performance -- Cordyceps supports energy and stamina and is particularly noted for athletes or anyone seeking a natural boost for workouts or sustained activity during long days.

5. Gut Health -- The more established benefits surrounding mushrooms are tied to their richness in prebiotic fibers, which keep the microbiome healthy by giving beneficial microbes the food they need to stay alive. Note: eating the whole mushroom is the only way to obtain these prebiotic fibers — supplements may not provide this benefit.

6. Cancer Supportive Care -- Reishi contains approximately 400 different bioactive compounds, among which triterpenoids and polysaccharides are the two major active anti-cancer constituents. Triterpenoids are recognized for anti-inflammatory and antitumor activities, while polysaccharides activate macrophages and natural

killer cells, supporting immune surveillance and tumor elimination. Reishi is increasingly used for symptom control by cancer patients. (Memorial Sloan Kettering Cancer Center / PMC, 2024)

7. Growing Market & Scientific Validation -- The global functional mushroom market was valued at approximately $31.71 billion in 2023 and is projected to reach $65.83 billion by 2030 — a compound annual growth rate of 11.2%, significantly outpacing many traditional supplement categories. Consumer adoption has reached 37% of surveyed consumers reporting consumption of mushroom-enhanced foods and beverages.

> *Historical note: Reishi has been used in traditional Chinese medicine since at least 206 BC. It is now listed in the American Herbal Pharmacopoeia, the Chinese Pharmacopoeia, and the Therapeutic Compendium, and is widely used as an adjuvant in the treatment of various cancers.*

The Cons

1. Most Research Still Preliminary -- While some of the claimed benefits of functional mushrooms have research support, most of the research has been conducted in animal models. More robust human clinical trials are needed before definitive conclusions can be drawn. Observational studies often have limitations and do not offer conclusive evidence.

2. No FDA Oversight of Health Claims -- While producers must follow FDA guidelines to ensure product safety, the FDA does not test or validate the purported health claims of functional mushroom products. Consumers must exercise their own due diligence.

3. Lack of Industry Standardization -- The current lack of standardization and regulation in the functional mushroom industry means that product quality and potency vary widely. Without clear

guidelines, verifying the consistency and accuracy of health claims is difficult. Just because a product is natural does not automatically mean it is effective or safe.

4. Supplement Form vs. Whole Food -- Eating the whole mushroom is the only way to obtain prebiotic fibers — the most established nutritional benefit. Processed supplements may not deliver the same value as whole food consumption. Consumers should not assume that a capsule or powder is equivalent to the whole food.

5. Drug Interactions & Contraindications -- Before trying functional mushrooms, it is important to consult a healthcare professional, as they may cause side effects or interact with medications. Key interaction risks include:

- Blood thinners (e.g., warfarin): Reishi may enhance anticoagulant effects
- Immunosuppressive medications: mushrooms' immune-stimulating properties may counteract these drugs
- Diabetes medications: some mushrooms may lower blood sugar, creating additive effects
- Blood pressure medications: potential for additive blood pressure-lowering effects

6. Allergic Reactions & Contamination Risk -- The main safety risk comes from allergic reactions or product contamination. Functional mushrooms have a short shelf life of one to three days due to high water content, making post-harvest transportation and storage critical. Quality control in the supply chain — particularly from international sources — is an ongoing concern.

Caution: Some functional mushroom products on the market combine multiple mushroom species with other herbs and supplements. These combination products carry additional interaction risks that are not always well-studied.

Smart Consumer Guidance

- Look for third-party tested supplements bearing the USP or NSF certification seal.
- Consult NatMed.com or speak with a pharmacist to check for drug-supplement interactions.
- When possible, consume whole mushrooms (cooked) rather than relying solely on supplements.
- Always consult a physician or registered dietitian before adding functional mushrooms to a health regimen — especially for anyone managing chronic conditions, taking prescription medications, or undergoing cancer treatment.
- Be skeptical of products making extravagant health claims without published human clinical trial data to back them up.

Shilajit & "Ancient Remedy" Marketing

Shilajit is a natural substance found mainly in the Himalayas, formed over centuries by the gradual decomposition of certain plants by the action of microorganisms. It is one of the oldest and most revered herbo-mineral compounds in Ayurvedic medicine, associated with potent antioxidant and anti-inflammatory effects. Its main active component is fulvic acid. It also contains humic acid, trace elements, minerals, and vitamins — making it a complex, variable, and location-dependent substance.

What it is NOT: Shilajit is not a drug, not FDA-approved for any medical condition, and not a standardized pharmaceutical product. Its composition varies significantly by geographic origin, processing method, and manufacturer.

The "Ancient Remedy" Marketing Context

Shilajit is heavily marketed using its Ayurvedic heritage. It is described in ancient Sanskrit texts as a rasayana (rejuvenator) and maharasa (super-vitalizer). Traditional health benefits attributed to it include increased longevity, rejuvenation, and arresting aging. These ancient claims carry real cultural weight — but are being commercially weaponized far beyond what modern science supports.

The vast majority of published research on shilajit originates from India and other Eastern institutions — which is appropriate given its origins — but this geographic concentration of research also means the findings have received less independent international replication than would be required for mainstream clinical adoption.

Red flag language to watch for: "Himalayan miracle," "ancient superfood," "thousands of years of proof," "master mineral," "the destroyer of weakness." These are marketing phrases, not clinical evidence. Longevity of use is not the same as scientific validation.

Areas Where Research Shows Promise

1. Cognitive Function & Neuroprotection -- Recent investigations point to medical applications toward the control of cognitive disorders associated with aging and cognitive stimulation. Fulvic acid, the main active principle, blocks tau protein self-aggregation — the same pathological process central to Alzheimer's disease — opening a potential avenue for therapeutic research.

A 2012 clinical study of individuals with probable Alzheimer's disease reported a slower rate of cognitive decline over 24 weeks in the shilajit-treated group compared to placebo — a promising but preliminary finding that requires larger trials to confirm.

2. Muscle Strength & Exercise Recovery -- A double-blind, placebo-controlled study found that 8 weeks of purified shilajit supplementation at 500 mg per day promoted the retention of maximal muscular strength following a fatiguing exercise protocol and produced favorable muscle and connective tissue adaptations — suggesting potential benefit for physical performance and recovery.

3. Bone Health (Postmenopausal Women) -- A rigorous 48-week randomized, double-blind, placebo-controlled trial of 60 postmenopausal women with osteopenia found that bone mineral density of the lumbar spine and femoral neck progressively decreased in the placebo group but was dose-dependently preserved with shilajit extract supplementation. Markers of bone turnover, inflammation, and oxidative stress also improved significantly in the supplemented groups compared to placebo. This is one of the strongest clinical studies supporting shilajit's use.

4. Chronic Fatigue, Altitude Sickness & Infertility -- A 2024 systematic review of 15 studies involving 1,254 participants covering conditions including chronic fatigue syndrome, high-altitude sickness, cognitive decline, and infertility found encouraging results across most trials. Adverse events were generally mild — gastrointestinal discomfort and headache — transient and self-resolving. No serious adverse events were reported across the included studies.

5. Antioxidant & Anti-Inflammatory Activity -- Shilajit is associated with antioxidant and anti-inflammatory effects via modulation of the NF-kB and Nrf2/HO-1 signaling pathways. It has been shown to reduce markers of inflammation and oxidative stress, and to improve glutathione (GSH) levels in type 2 diabetics.

The Risks — Where Serious Caution Is Warranted

1. Heavy Metal Contamination — A Documented Public Health Risk

This is the most serious concern with shilajit and cannot be overstated. A 2024 review of recent research found that raw shilajit often contains toxic or potentially toxic materials. A 2025 study (BMC Chemistry) found that some commercially sold shilajit supplements actually contained higher levels of the toxic heavy metal thallium than the raw, unprocessed variety.

CRITICAL: Thallium is a potent neurotoxin. Heavy metal contamination — including thallium, arsenic, and lead — in unprocessed or counterfeit shilajit products is a documented, real-world danger. This is not a theoretical risk. Only purified, third-party tested products from reputable brands should ever be used.

2. No FDA Regulation of Health Claims -- The FDA does not regulate dietary supplements as strictly as pharmaceuticals, which leads to significant variation in quality control and safety profiles across brands. The FDA does not test or validate the health claims made by supplement manufacturers. Consumers cannot know with certainty what they are taking unless the product has independent third-party certification.

3. Variable Composition — No Standardization. Shilajit is a naturally occurring mixture, meaning no two batches are identical. Location, plant life, temperature, altitude, and processing methods all change its composition, nutritional makeup, color, and taste. This makes it virtually impossible to guarantee consistent quality or determine a universally safe dosage without standardized, tested products.

4. Drug Interactions -- Shilajit may interact with several categories of medications due to its complex chemical composition and hormonal effects:

- Antidiabetic medications: may enhance blood sugar-lowering effects, requiring glucose monitoring
- Antihypertensive medications: possible additive blood pressure-lowering effects
- Hormone-modulating drugs: shilajit may influence testosterone and other hormone levels
- Blood thinners: potential interaction due to its iron content and effects on platelet function

5. Overstated and Unsubstantiated Claims -- Traditional and emerging scientific data suggest shilajit may offer multiple health benefits — but these claims are not universally supported by clinical

data. Most benefits are speculative or based on small-scale, short-term studies. Common overblown claims include:

- "Reverses aging" — no clinical evidence in humans
- "Boosts testosterone dramatically" — small studies only; effects modest
- "Cures infertility" — preliminary findings in small groups, not replicated at scale
- "Detoxifies the body" — ironic given the contamination risks of unprocessed shilajit
- "Proven for thousands of years" — traditional use is not a substitute for clinical trials

Key Takeaways for Community Education

- Shilajit has a legitimate place in traditional Ayurvedic medicine. That history is being commercially exploited with claims that go far beyond current evidence.
- Promising research exists, particularly for cognitive protection, muscle recovery, and bone health in postmenopausal women — but most studies are small and require larger replication.
- Thallium, arsenic, and lead have been documented in commercial shilajit products. Only use purified, standardized, third-party certified products. Heavy metal contamination is the #1 safety concern.
- A healthcare provider should guide product selection. "Natural" does not mean safe. Only buy from reputable, recommended brands.
- Drug interactions are real, particularly with diabetes, blood pressure, and hormone-related medications.
- "Ancient remedy" and "Himalayan miracle" language is marketing, not medicine. There is no FDA validation of claims.
- Especially critical for patients managing chronic conditions or taking prescription medications, always disclose to your physician.

How to Read a Supplement Label

Why This Matters -- When it comes to dietary supplements, the label is not just a marketing tool — it is a legal document. The FDA regulates what information must appear on supplement packaging and how it must be presented. However, dietary supplements fall under the Dietary Supplement Health and Education Act (DSHEA), which treats supplements as a category of food. This means supplements do NOT require FDA preapproval before going to market. The burden of evaluation falls largely on the consumer — making label literacy an essential life skill.

Bottom line -- Knowing how to read a supplement label is one of the most practical health literacy skills a consumer can develop. This guide walks through every section — from the Supplement Facts panel to third-party seals to red flag marketing language.

The 5 Required Elements on Every Supplement Label -- FDA regulations mandate that all dietary supplement containers include five essential label statements. Missing any of these elements means the product may be considered misbranded under federal law:

1. must appear on the front panel of the package, clearly identifying the product type (e.g., "Herbal Supplement," "Vitamin Supplement")"Dietary Supplement" identity statement —
2. how much is in the package (e.g., "60 capsules" or "30 servings")Net quantity of contents —
3. the standardized nutritional information box — the heart of the label Supplement Facts panel —
4. inactive ingredients like binders, fillers, coatings, and flavors, listed outside the Supplement Facts box Other Ingredients list —
5. including a U.S. contact point for adverse event reporting (required by law since the 2006 Consumer Protection Act) Manufacturer name and address —

How to Read the Supplement Facts Panel -- This is the most important part of the label. Every amount listed is per serving — not per container. This is where many consumers are misled.

Serving Size -- Located at the very top of the Supplement Facts box. All ingredient amounts that follow are based on this serving size. A bottle of 120 capsules with a serving size of 4 means only 30 servings per bottle — not 120.

Amount Per Serving -- Lists each ingredient with its quantity in milligrams (mg), micrograms (mcg), International Units (IU), or other units. Look at the actual dose — not just the ingredient name. A label listing 10 mg of a compound that requires 500 mg to be clinically effective is essentially useless.

% Daily Value (%DV) -- Shows how much of a nutrient one serving provides relative to the recommended daily intake. A dagger symbol (†) means no Daily Value has been established for that ingredient — common with herbs and proprietary compounds. Be wary of nutrients listed at more than 100% DV, as this may exceed what your body needs from your entire diet combined.

The Bold Line -- A thick bold line divides the panel. Above it are ingredients with established Daily Values (vitamins, minerals). Below it are "other dietary ingredients" without established DVs — often herbs, botanicals, and proprietary compounds. These are still required to show their quantity in mg.

"Other Ingredients" (Outside the Box) -- Listed below or beside the Supplement Facts panel — not inside it. These are inactive ingredients: binders, coatings, fillers, colorings, and flavors. This is where allergens (soy, wheat, shellfish, dairy) must also be declared. Read this section if you have food sensitivities or allergies.

Watch out for "Proprietary Blend": When a label lists a "Proprietary Blend" with a total weight but no individual ingredient amounts, you cannot know if each component is present in a therapeutically meaningful dose. This is a common marketing tactic — and a consumer protection gap.

Understanding the Three Types of Legal Health Claims **--** The FDA regulates three major categories of claims on supplement labels. Understanding the difference protects you from being misled.

1. Structure/Function Claims (Most Common) -- These explain how a nutrient supports normal body functions. They do NOT require FDA approval but must be accompanied by the required disclaimer. Examples:

- ALLOWED: "Supports immune health" / "Promotes bone strength" / "Supports energy production"
- NOT ALLOWED: "Treats arthritis" / "Cures insomnia" / "Prevents cancer"

2. Nutrient Content Claims -- Regulated descriptions of the level of a nutrient in the product. Examples: "High in vitamin C," "Excellent source of calcium." These are allowed but regulated.

3. Health Claims (Most Restricted) -- These link a nutrient to reducing the risk of a specific disease. They require FDA authorization and are very limited. Currently authorized examples include: calcium and vitamin D for osteoporosis, folate for neural tube defects, and soluble fiber for heart disease.

The Required FDA Disclaimer -- Every supplement label that makes a structure/function claim must include this exact disclaimer, with adequate prominence:

> *This statement has not been evaluated by the Food and Drug Administration. This product is not intended to diagnose, treat, cure, or prevent any disease.*

If a product makes health claims but does NOT carry this disclaimer, it may be in violation of FDA regulations — and that is a serious red flag. Conversely, seeing this disclaimer is a normal and expected part of a compliant supplement label, not a sign that the product is dangerous.

Third-Party Certification Seals — Your Best Consumer Protection

Because the FDA does not pre-approve supplements, third-party certification is the most meaningful quality assurance a consumer can find on a label. These independent organizations verify that: the ingredients listed on the label match what is actually inside; there are no harmful contaminants like heavy metals or microbes; and the product was manufactured in a GMP-certified facility.

USP Verified -- The U.S. Pharmacopeia (USP) is a nonprofit scientific organization with over 200 years of history. Products bearing the USP Verified mark must meet standards for: Identity (contains what the label says), Potency (accurately represented through shelf life), Purity (free of contaminants), and Performance (dissolves properly for absorption). Manufacturers undergo routine site inspections and product retesting. Trusted brands with broad USP verification include Nature Made and Kirkland Signature (Costco).

NSF Certified -- NSF International conducts product testing in its own accredited laboratories to confirm label accuracy and absence of harmful contaminants. It also registers the manufacturing facility and conducts annual audits with periodic retesting. NSF certifies products against NSF/ANSI 173 — the only American National Standard for dietary supplement ingredients.

NSF Certified for Sport -- Everything in NSF Certified, plus screening for over 270 substances banned by major athletic organizations including the NFL, MLB, PGA, and LPGA. Recommended by USADA for competitive athletes subject to drug testing.

Informed Choice / Informed Sport -- Tests for banned substances and verifies label accuracy. Informed Sport is the athlete-grade program, testing every batch. Free mobile apps allow athletes to scan barcodes and verify batch-specific certification.

ConsumerLab -- An independent lab that publishes test results publicly online. ConsumerLab holds all product forms — including gummies — to the same high standards, unlike some other programs. ConsumerLab frequently finds that the highest-priced supplements are not the highest-quality ones.

> *Important: Certification is product-specific (SKU-specific). One flavor or formula of a brand may be certified while another is not. Always verify the exact product you are purchasing, not just the brand name.*

Red Flags & Meaningless Marketing Terms to Ignore
Deceptive Marketing Language

- "Pharmaceutical Grade" -- there is no legal or regulatory definition for this term in supplements; it is meaningless.
- "Clinically Prove" -- requires verification. Ask: proven by whom? In how many people? Published where?
- "Natural" -- not regulated. A product can be labeled "natural" and still contain additives, allergens, or ineffective doses.
- "Doctor Formulated" -- not a regulated claim; does not indicate FDA review or third-party testing.
- "Proprietary Blend" -- hides individual ingredient amounts. You cannot determine if meaningful doses are present.

Fake or Misleading Certification Language

- "USP quality" or "USP tested" without the actual circular USP Verified mark — these phrases do not equal USP verification.
- "Third-Party Tested" without naming the third party, this is meaningless. Always look for a named certification organization and its seal.
- Products sold through unauthorized Amazon sellers or discount sites may display counterfeit verification marks. Check for

misspellings, poor label quality, or certification numbers that do not match the official database.

Illegal Claims

- Any claim that a supplement treats, cures, diagnoses, or prevents a specific disease — without FDA authorization — is illegal under federal law and a serious red flag.
- Examples of illegal claims: "Cures diabetes," "Eliminates cancer," "Reverses Alzheimer's"

Quick Reference — Supplement Label Checklist

Use this checklist every time you evaluate a supplement:

- Does the front panel say "Dietary Supplement"?
- Is there a complete Supplement Facts panel with serving size, ingredient names, and quantities in specific units (mg, mcg, IU)?
- What is the actual dose per ingredient — is it a therapeutic amount based on research?
- Is there a "Proprietary Blend" hiding individual doses? If so, consider this a concern.
- Are inactive ingredients (Other Ingredients) listed — any allergens present?
- Does the label carry a named third-party certification seal (USP, NSF, Informed Choice, ConsumerLab)?
- If health claims are made, is the required FDA disclaimer present?
- Are there any disease treatment claims (treat, cure, diagnose, prevent)? If yes — red flag.
- Is the manufacturer's name and U.S. contact information present?
- Has a pharmacist, physician, or registered dietitian been consulted before purchase?

Chapter 6

Brain Health Marketing & Cognitive Claims

Brain Health Without the Hype: How to Protect Your Mind in a World Full of Fear-Based Ads

If you feel as though you're being bombarded by ads promising to "reverse memory loss," "restore your brain in seconds," or reveal a "secret Harvard discovery," you're not imagining things.

There has been a sharp rise in fear-driven marketing aimed at adults who are rightly concerned about brain health. These ads often look scientific, sound urgent, and lean heavily on emotion. What they rarely provide is solid evidence.

Let's separate what actually supports brain health from what's simply clever marketing.

Why These Ads Feel So Aggressive: Most brain-health ads follow the same script:

A dramatic warning about memory loss
A claim that doctors or scientists are "hiding the truth"
A promise of fast, effortless results
A supplement, tonic, frequency, or "simple trick" as the solution

This style of messaging is not designed to educate. It is designed to trigger fear, urgency, and insecurity, which makes people more likely to buy before asking questions. Real science does not need secrecy, countdown clocks, or miracle language.

What Brain-Health Science Actually Supports: The most reliable research on cognitive health is consistent and unglamorous. Brain health is built the same way good health has always been built: steadily, not instantly. The true foundations of brain health include:

Sleep – Consistent, quality sleep is one of the strongest protectors of memory and cognitive function. No supplement overrides chronic sleep deprivation.

Vascular Health – The brain depends on healthy blood flow. Blood pressure, blood sugar, and cholesterol all matter. What protects the heart also protects the brain.

Movement – Regular movement—especially walking, balance work, and light strength training—supports blood flow, mood, and neuroplasticity.

Mental and Social Engagement – Conversation, reading, teaching, learning, and meaningful connection help preserve cognitive reserve. Isolation accelerates decline; engagement slows it.

Stress Regulation – Chronic stress and elevated cortisol damage memory centers in the brain. Calm is not a luxury—it is protective.

Where Supplements Fit (and Where They Don't): Some supplements may support general wellness or help fill nutritional gaps. They may offer modest support for some people.

They do not:

Reverse dementia

Repair damaged neurons on demand

Replace sleep, movement, or medical care

Any product claiming otherwise is selling hope before selling evidence.

A Simple Filter for Brain-Health Claims: Before trusting a product or program, ask:

Are claims cautious and realistic, or dramatic and absolute?
Are ingredients and dosages clearly disclosed?
Are peer-reviewed studies cited—not just testimonials?
Does it encourage healthy habits, or promise results without effort?

If fear comes before facts, it's time to disengage.

The human brain remains adaptable well into later life. It responds best to consistency, nourishment, movement, connection, and peace, not panic.

Discernment protects peace. Peace protects the mind.

Disclaimer: This article is for educational purposes only and is not intended as medical advice. Always consult a qualified healthcare professional regarding individual health concerns.

Chapter 7

How to Spot Health Misinformation

What It Is

Misinformation is false or misleading information shared without intent to deceive. Disinformation is false information spread deliberately to deceive. Both cause real harm, but disinformation is increasingly weaponized for political purposes.

Why It Is an Urgent Crisis

In 2025, the American Psychological Association released a consensus statement identifying health misinformation as one of the most urgent threats to public health. The World Health Organization has labeled this an "infodemic" — an overabundance of information, both accurate and inaccurate, that makes it hard for people to find trustworthy guidance when they need it most.

Much like an infectious pathogen, misinformation spreads quickly, silently, and with significant downstream harm. — University of Nebraska Medical Center, December 2025

How It Spreads

Key Psychological Drivers

- The Illusory Truth Effect: people tend to believe information they encounter repeatedly, even if it is false — one of the strongest drivers of misinformation uptake.
- Emotional amplification: fear, anger, surprise, and outrage dramatically increase the likelihood of sharing content online.

- Identity and belonging: people share information because it aligns with their identity, reinforces group belonging, or offers a sense of control and meaning.
- Susceptibility is linked less to intelligence and more to mistrust of institutions, government, or healthcare — one of the most potent accelerants of misinformation.

The Role of Social Media

Health misinformation is often divisive. Wellness influencers are known to undermine public health authorities and erode public trust in credible health experts. Many people instead trust alternative sources that spread misinformation — creating a dangerous paradox: the mistrust fueled by misinformation enables its continued spread.

Platform Accountability Rollbacks

- In January 2025, Meta announced it would drop independent third-party fact-checkers, stating they led to "too much censorship" — even though Facebook was already a major source of health misinformation.
- Elon Musk reduced X's (formerly Twitter's) content moderation team and has publicly voiced opposition to content moderation.
- Research shows only 16% of COVID-19 misinformation on Facebook carried a warning label at the height of the pandemic.

Real-World Harms

- Cancer prevention and treatment: misleading social media content leads patients to abandon evidence-based treatments in favor of influencer-backed alternatives.
- Mental health: misinformation downplays the seriousness of mental health conditions.
- Supplements: promotes unregulated products claiming to address everything from weight loss to reversing aging.
- Vaccines and public health: during the pandemic, misinformation led people to decline vaccines, reject public health measures, and use unproven treatments.

- Violence: health misinformation has led to harassment and violence against health workers and other essential personnel.

Who Is Most Affected

Research shows that perception of substantial health misinformation on social media is associated with lower trust in the U.S. healthcare system. Among those who reported high trust in the healthcare system, 65.1% perceived less health misinformation on social media, while 34.9% perceived substantial misinformation. Marginalized communities are disproportionately harmed.

What Can Be Done -- Systemic Approach

Combating misinformation requires a systematic approach similar to curbing infectious disease:

- Finding and containing the source
- Proactively identifying the most vulnerable
- "Immunizing" the population against false claims through clear educational resources

It cannot be left to voluntary, individual efforts.

Trusted Messengers

The U.S. Surgeon General's Community Toolkit for Addressing Health Misinformation (published in 2021) provides guidance specifically for health care providers, educators, librarians, faith leaders, and trusted community members to understand, identify, and stop the spread of health misinformation in their communities.

Media and Platform Recommendations

- Train journalists and editors to recognize, correct, and avoid amplifying misinformation.
- Proactively address the public's questions with context to avoid skewed perceptions.
- Strengthen monitoring and early detection of misinformation "super-spreaders."
- Australia is introducing substantial fines for platforms that fail to prevent the spread of misinformation — a potential model for other nations.

Part II

Insurance and Financial Protection

Chapter 8

Social Security: Strategy, Not Guesswork

For many Americans, Social Security is the single most stable retirement income stream they will ever receive. Yet it is often claimed with less analysis than a cell phone contract. After decades in insurance practice and as a Registered Social Security Analyst, I can say confidently: most mistakes are not malicious or careless. They are rushed.

Part I – Common Claiming Mistakes

Claiming at 62 Without Running the Math – Age 62 is the earliest eligibility age for retirement benefits. For many, it becomes the default.

What is often overlooked:
Benefits are permanently reduced for early claiming.
Reductions can exceed 25–30% depending on Full Retirement Age (FRA).
Longevity risk is underestimated.

If you live into your 80s or 90s, early claiming can result in hundreds of thousands of dollars in lost lifetime income.

Ignoring Spousal and Survivor Coordination – Married couples frequently claim independently rather than strategically.

Overlooked issues:
Survivor benefits are based on the higher earner's benefit.
Claiming early can permanently reduce survivor income.
Coordination matters more than speed.

Failing to Review Earnings Record – Errors occur. If your earnings record is incorrect:
Your benefit will be calculated incorrectly.
The burden of correction is on you.

Waiting until retirement to review records reduces your correction window.

Not Understanding the Earnings Test – If claiming before Full Retirement Age while still working:
Benefits may be temporarily withheld if earnings exceed annual limits.
Misunderstanding this creates unnecessary frustration.
The withheld benefits are not "lost," but many do not understand the adjustment mechanism.

Assuming Social Security Is "Going Broke" – This narrative causes premature claiming. Social Security faces long-term funding challenges, but complete disappearance is highly unlikely. Legislative adjustments historically preserve core benefits. Fear-based claiming decisions can permanently reduce income.

Part II – Optimization Strategies

Optimization is not about "gaming the system." It is about understanding how the rules work.

1 Understanding Full Retirement Age (FRA) – FRA depends on year of birth.
Claiming at FRA:
Eliminates early reduction
Allows full earnings without earnings test penalties

2 Delayed Retirement Credits – For each year you delay beyond FRA (up to age 70):

Benefits increase approximately 8% per year.

The increase is permanent.

For healthy individuals with longevity in their family, this can dramatically increase lifetime income — and survivor protection.

3 Coordinated Spousal Strategy – For couples:

Higher earner may delay to maximize survivor protection.

Lower earner may claim earlier depending on household needs.

Coordination can add meaningful lifetime value.

4 Tax Awareness – Up to 85% of Social Security benefits may be taxable depending on combined income. Planning withdrawals from retirement accounts strategically can reduce taxation impact.

5 Longevity Planning – Average life expectancy is not your life expectancy. If one spouse lives into their 90s, the claiming decision becomes a long-term inflation-adjusted income strategy.

Part III – Strategy Blended With Caution

Over the years, I have seen patterns repeat.

- A healthy 62-year-old claims early because "I might as well get it now." Ten years later, with medical needs increasing and inflation affecting daily expenses, the permanently reduced benefit becomes a source of regret.

- A widow discovers that her spouse claimed early, not realizing it would reduce her survivor benefit for the rest of her life.

- A high earner delays properly, increasing not only their own benefit but providing a stronger financial floor for the surviving spouse.

These are not abstract scenarios. They are recurring realities. Social Security decisions are permanent. You are making a lifetime income choice in a single filing action.

Key Takeaways

Early claiming permanently reduces benefits.

Spousal coordination is critical.

Survivor benefits depend on the higher earner's decision.

Delaying can meaningfully increase lifetime income.

Fear-driven decisions often cost more than patience.

What You Should Do Next

Create a *my Social Security* account and review your earnings record.

Determine your Full Retirement Age.

Estimate benefits at 62, FRA, and 70.

If married, evaluate both records together.

Consider longevity, health, and survivor protection — not just immediate cash flow. Seek analysis before filing. Filing is easy. Reversing is limited.

Professional Disclaimer: Social Security rules are complex and subject to legislative change. Benefit optimization depends on individual earnings history, marital status, tax considerations, and longevity assumptions. Readers should consult qualified professionals before filing for benefits.

Chapter 9

ACA and Premium Tax Credit Realities

When Estimated Income Becomes Expensive: The Affordable Care Act (ACA) marketplace was designed to expand access to health insurance through income-based premium tax credits. In theory, it is straightforward. In practice, it requires precision.

Unlike Medicare, which is primarily age-based, ACA eligibility and subsidy amounts are tied to projected Modified Adjusted Gross Income (MAGI). That projection determines whether you receive assistance — and how much. And that projection must later be reconciled with reality.

Part I – The Most Common ACA Mistakes

1 Underestimating Income to Increase Subsidy – The temptation is understandable. A lower projected income results in a larger premium tax credit. The monthly premium drops. The policy becomes affordable. But when tax season arrives, the IRS reconciles actual income against the estimate.

If actual income exceeds the projected amount:
A portion — or all — of the subsidy may have to be repaid.
Repayment caps vary by income level.
Above certain thresholds, full repayment may be required.
The relief felt during the year can become a shock at tax time.

2 Failing to Report Mid-Year Income Changes – Income is not static.

Common mid-year changes:

New employment
Retirement account withdrawals
Business growth
Sale of property
Required Minimum Distributions (RMDs)

If these are not reported to the Marketplace, subsidy calculations remain incorrect.

3 Misunderstanding MAGI – Modified Adjusted Gross Income includes:

Wages
Business income
Social Security (taxable portion)
Interest and dividends
Capital gains
Certain retirement withdrawals

Many assume only "salary" counts. It does not.

4 Ignoring the Subsidy Cliff (Historical & Legislative Changes) – In past years, exceeding certain income thresholds eliminated subsidies entirely. Legislative changes temporarily modified this structure, but subsidy rules can change with future legislation. Planning must consider:

Current law
Potential expiration of temporary provisions
Income volatility

5 Assuming ACA Is Permanent Retirement Coverage – ACA coverage is transitional. It may serve:

Early retirees (62–64)
Self-employed individuals

Those between employer plans
But it is not a substitute for Medicare planning once eligible.

Part II – Strategic ACA Planning

The ACA is not just an insurance enrollment decision. It is a tax planning strategy.

1 Income Range Targeting – Instead of guessing income, strategic planning identifies:

Lower boundary (Medicaid eligibility threshold in some states)
Upper boundary (where subsidies phase out or repayment risk increases)

This creates a planning corridor.

2 Coordinating Retirement Withdrawals – For early retirees:

Traditional IRA withdrawals increase MAGI.
Roth withdrawals typically do not.
Capital gains affect MAGI.

Timing withdrawals strategically can preserve subsidy eligibility.

3 Business Owners and S-Corps – Business owners must:

Project net business income carefully.
Consider reasonable compensation rules.
Avoid artificially suppressing income solely to increase subsidy.

Aggressive manipulation invites audit risk.

4 Reporting Changes Promptly – Income changes should be updated through the Marketplace as they occur — not deferred until tax filing. This reduces reconciliation surprises.

Part III – Cautionary Patterns

I have seen families enjoy extremely low monthly premiums during the year — only to discover at tax time that their actual income exceeded projections. The resulting repayment undermined the very financial stability they sought. I have also seen careful planning — strategic retirement withdrawals, disciplined income projections, prompt reporting — produce predictable, manageable outcomes with minimal reconciliation stress. The difference is not luck. It is discipline.

Key Takeaways

ACA subsidies are advance tax credits, not discounts.
Income projection accuracy matters.
MAGI includes more than wages.
Mid-year reporting reduces tax shock.
Strategic income planning can preserve affordability.

What You Should Do Next

Review your current year income projection.

Identify possible income volatility (business, investments, distributions).

Coordinate with your tax professional before year-end withdrawals.

Report income changes promptly to the Marketplace.

Prepare for reconciliation — do not ignore IRS Form 8962.

Professional Disclaimer: ACA eligibility and subsidy calculations depend on federal and state regulations, tax law, and individual financial circumstances. Readers should consult licensed insurance and tax professionals before making enrollment or income planning decisions.

Chapter 10

Trusts: Myths vs. Practical Realities

What a Trust Does — and What It Does Not Do: Few financial tools are as misunderstood as trusts. The word itself carries weight. It suggests protection. Permanence. Even invincibility. Terms like "bulletproof trust" are marketed as if legal documents can eliminate all risk. They cannot.

Part I – Revocable vs. Irrevocable Trusts

Revocable Living Trust

What It Does:

- Avoids probate in many cases
- Provides continuity in incapacity
- Allows asset management flexibility
- Can simplify estate administration

What It Does NOT Do:

- Does not shield assets from creditors
- Does not protect assets from lawsuits
- Does not protect assets from Medicaid spend-down
- Does not reduce estate taxes for most individuals

Revocable means changeable. If you control it, it is generally still considered yours for liability purposes.

Irrevocable Trust

What It Does:

Transfers ownership out of your name
May provide asset protection (if properly structured)
May assist in Medicaid planning
May reduce estate tax exposure (for larger estates)

What It Does NOT Do:

Guarantee protection if created during crisis
Bypass Medicaid lookback rules
Automatically eliminate tax consequences
Remove the need for disciplined planning

Irrevocable means you surrender control. That is not a small decision.

Part II – Medicaid Trust Myths: The most common misconceptions I encounter:

Myth #1:"I can move assets into a trust when I need nursing home care."

Reality: Medicaid has a five-year lookback period. Transfers made within that window can trigger penalty periods.

Myth #2: "A trust makes me ineligible for nothing."

Reality: Improperly structured trusts can create unintended tax or eligibility consequences.

Myth #3: "All trusts are the same."

Reality: Trust language, trustee authority, funding timing, and state law all matter.

Part III – Practical Application: Trust planning works best when:

Done years before care is needed
Coordinated with long-term care strategy
Integrated with estate planning

Reviewed periodically

Trusts are tools. They are not shields against poor timing.

Key Takeaways

Revocable trusts avoid probate — not liability.

Irrevocable trusts require surrender of control.

Medicaid planning requires early action.

“Bulletproof” marketing language is misleading.

Legal structure must align with financial reality.

What You Should Do Next

Determine what type of trust you currently have (if any).

Confirm whether it is funded properly.

Review trustee designations.

Understand Medicaid lookback implications.

Coordinate trust planning with LTC strategy.

Professional Disclaimer: Trust planning involves state-specific legal and tax considerations. Readers should consult qualified estate planning attorneys and tax professionals before establishing or modifying trust structures.

Chapter 11

S Corp. Income Strategy

Salary, Distributions, and Discipline – Many small business owners hear some version of this claim: "You can pay yourself less salary and take the rest as distributions to save on taxes." There is truth here — but also risk.

Part I – The Structure
An S-Corporation allows:
Salary (subject to payroll taxes)
Distributions (not subject to self-employment tax)

The IRS requires "reasonable compensation." That phrase is not decorative.

Part II – Common Mistakes
1 Artificially Low Salary
Setting salary unreasonably low to maximize distributions invites audit scrutiny. Factors considered:
Industry standards
Role performed
Time devoted to business
Comparable compensation

2 Ignoring State Tax and Compliance – Some states impose franchise or margin taxes. Compliance errors can erase federal savings.

3 Confusing Cash Flow with Taxable Income – Distributions are not "free money." They reduce basis and interact with overall tax reporting.

Part III – Strategic Discipline: Proper S-Corp strategy includes:
Reasonable salary analysis
Quarterly estimated tax planning
Retirement contribution coordination
Health insurance premium treatment
Long-term planning alignment
Tax efficiency should not override compliance.

Key Takeaways
S-Corp structure can reduce self-employment taxes.
Reasonable compensation is mandatory.
Documentation protects you.
Aggressive manipulation increases audit risk.

What You Should Do Next
Review your salary-to-distribution ratio.
Document how salary was determined.
Coordinate with a CPA annually.
Align retirement and health insurance planning with corporate structure.

Professional Disclaimer: S-Corp taxation involves complex federal and state regulations. Business owners should consult qualified tax professionals before modifying compensation structures.

Chapter 12

Investment Red Flags: When Yield Outpaces Prudence

Investment opportunities promising unusually high returns often carry unusually high risk. The phrase "guaranteed 8% or 9%" should prompt careful examination.

Part I – High-Yield Reality: If traditional fixed-income markets yield 3–5%, a consistent 9% return requires explanation.

Questions to ask:
What is the underlying asset?
How is return generated?
What happens in downturns?
Is principal guaranteed? By whom?
Is there SEC registration?

Part II – Common Warning Signs
Urgency-based marketing
Limited-time opportunity claims
Complex structure with unclear cash flow
Reliance on future development success
Heavy emphasis on testimonials

Part III – Due Diligence Discipline: Before investing:
Verify registration (SEC, state regulators).
Request audited financial statements.
Understand liquidity restrictions.
Assess concentration risk.

Avoid investing funds you cannot afford to lose.

Cautionary Pattern – In my experience, high-yield offerings often attract individuals seeking stability in retirement — precisely the group least able to absorb capital loss. Yield without transparency is speculation.

Key Takeaways

High returns require high explanation.
Transparency matters more than promises.
Liquidity restrictions increase risk.
Diversification protects stability.

What You Should Do Next

Re-evaluate any investment promising above-market yield.
Request documentation before transferring funds.
Consult independent advisors.
Avoid concentration in single offerings.

Professional Disclaimer: Investment decisions carry risk, including loss of principal. This material is educational and not investment advice. Readers should consult licensed financial professionals before investing.

Part III

Consumer Defense and Legal Awareness

Chapter 13

Writing Demand Letters That Get Attention

Professional, Precise, and Difficult to Ignore: When something goes wrong — a denied claim, a breached contract, a misapplied charge — emotion is natural. But emotion does not win disputes. Structure does. A demand letter is not a rant. It is not a threat. It is not a place to rehearse frustration. It is a documented record of facts, law, and requested remedy.

Part I – What Makes a Demand Letter Effective – An effective demand letter includes:

A clear timeline
Relevant documentation references
Specific contractual or statutory citations (if applicable)
A defined remedy request
A reasonable response deadline

It does not include:

Personal attacks
Unverifiable accusations
Excessive adjectives
Idle threats

Precision carries more force than anger.

Part II – Structural Framework – A disciplined demand letter generally follows this sequence:

1 Introduction – Identify parties and purpose
2 Timeline – Chronological, factual
3 Documentation – Referenced clearly
4 Legal/Contractual Basis – If applicable
5 Specific Demand – Dollar amount or corrective action
6 Deadline – Reasonable but firm
7 Notice of Further Action – Professional, not inflammatory

Part III – Why Tone Matters – A well-structured letter signals seriousness.

Companies respond differently to:
"I am furious and this is unacceptable..."
versus
"On January 14, 2026, the following occurred..."
Professional tone increases credibility.

Key Takeaways
Facts persuade more effectively than emotion.
Documentation is essential.
Structure increases leverage.
Professional tone improves response likelihood.

What You Should Do Next
Gather documentation before writing.
Create a chronological timeline.
Identify the specific remedy you seek.
Send via trackable delivery.
Retain copies.

Professional Disclaimer: This chapter provides general information regarding consumer correspondence and dispute documentation. It is not legal advice. Consult licensed attorneys for case-specific matters.

Chapter 14

Preserving Evidence in a Digital World

If It Is Not Preserved, It Is Often Lost – Many disputes are not lost because they lack merit. They are lost because documentation is incomplete. In the digital age, preservation requires intention.

Part I – Email and Metadata: – Emails contain:
Time stamps
Sender and recipient records
Attachments
Embedded metadata
Deleting or failing to archive emails weakens position.

Best practice:
Maintain digital folders
Export critical threads
Backup important communications

Part II – USPS and Delivery Confirmation: – Trackable mail provides:
Delivery confirmation
Date verification
Evidence of receipt
Electronic signatures are increasingly accepted in many jurisdictions, but requirements vary. Always verify local court or regulatory standards before relying solely on electronic proof.

Part III – Screenshots and Digital Records – When dealing with:

Online advertisements
Account portals
Policy documents

Capture:

Date-stamped screenshots
Full-page captures
Downloaded PDFs

Web content can change without notice.

Key Takeaways

Documentation must be intentional.
Preserve before conflict escalates.
Maintain digital backups.
Verify proof-of-delivery standards.

What You Should Do Next

Establish a digital document storage system.
Back up critical records.
Use trackable delivery for important correspondence.
Preserve evidence before filing complaints.

Professional Disclaimer: Evidence preservation standards vary by jurisdiction and matter type. Consult legal professionals for guidance specific to your case.

Chapter 15

Filing Regulatory Complaints Effectively

Understanding What They Can — and Cannot Do: Regulatory agencies exist to enforce standards. But they are not private attorneys. Understanding their scope prevents misplaced expectations.

Part I – Insurance Departments– State insurance departments:

Investigate compliance violations
Review claims handling practices
Enforce regulatory standards

They do not:

Automatically award damages
Replace civil litigation

Part II – State Bar Complaints – Disciplinary committees:

Investigate professional misconduct
Evaluate ethical violations
Impose sanctions where appropriate

They do not:

Recover client funds directly
Litigate civil disputes

Part III – Strategic Use of Complaints – Regulatory complaints are effective when:

Documentation is thorough
Timeline is clear
Allegations are specific
Emotional language is avoided

They are ineffective when used as emotional leverage.

Key Takeaways

Regulators enforce rules — they do not litigate for you.
Clear documentation strengthens complaints.
Professional tone improves credibility.
Escalation should be strategic, not reactive.

What You Should Do Next

Confirm the appropriate regulatory body.
Organize documentation before filing.
State facts clearly and chronologically.
Maintain copies of all submissions.

Professional Disclaimer: Regulatory processes vary by jurisdiction and industry. This material is informational and not legal advice.

Part IV

Technology and Personal Security

Chapter 16

Scam Calls and Phone Defense

Discipline Beats Technology Alone

Most scam calls are not sophisticated. They are persistent. What makes them effective is volume and urgency.

"Your account has been compromised."

"A warrant has been issued."

"This is your final notice."

The goal is emotional destabilization.

Part I – Why Scam Calls Work: They exploit:

Fear
Authority tone
Urgency
Confusion
Isolation

Scammers do not need most people to respond. They just need a small percentage.

Part II – Technical Defense Tools

1 Carrier-Level Blocking – Most carriers offer:

Call filtering
Spam labeling
Automatic blocking of known scam numbers

Enable these features.

2 Third-Party Blocking Services – Applications such as call filtering services:

Identify robocalls
Block repeat offenders
Reduce volume
Ensure settings remain enabled after system updates.

3 Voicemail Screening – Let unknown calls go to voicemail. Legitimate institutions will leave a message.

Part III – Behavioral Discipline: Technology helps. Behavior protects.

Never:
Provide personal information on inbound calls.
Confirm Social Security numbers.
Respond to urgent payment demands.

If concerned:
Hang up.
Call the institution directly using a verified number.

Key Takeaways
Scam calls rely on emotional pressure.
Let unknown calls go to voicemail.
Verify independently before responding.
Silence is often the safest response.

What You Should Do Next
Review carrier blocking settings.
Enable call filtering tools.
Remove your number from public listings if possible.
Establish a personal rule: never act during the first call.

Professional Disclaimer: Scam tactics evolve continuously. Readers should consult official government resources such as the FTC for updated guidance.

Chapter 17

Smart Devices & Privacy Protection

Convenience Has a Cost. Smart televisions. Voice assistants. Security cameras. Fitness trackers. Appliances connected to Wi-Fi. Convenience has expanded rapidly. So has data collection.

Part I – What Is Being Collected: Smart devices may collect:
Voice recordings
Viewing habits
Location data
Usage patterns
Contact information

Often, this data is used for targeted advertising. Sometimes, it is shared with third parties.

Part II – The Step-by-Step Privacy Action Plan

Step 1 – Change Default Passwords –
Use strong, unique passwords.
Avoid manufacturer defaults.

Step 2 – Enable Two-Factor Authentication
Where available, enable additional verification layers.

Step 3 – Review Privacy Settings Within device apps:

Disable unnecessary data sharing.
Opt out of targeted advertising.

Limit microphone access where possible.

Step 4 – Segment Your Network – If possible, Use separate Wi-Fi networks for smart devices and personal computers. This limits exposure if a device is compromised.

Step 5 – Update Firmware Regularly – Outdated software creates vulnerabilities.

Step 6 – Be Cautious With "Free" Apps – If the product is free, your data may be the product.

Key Takeaways

Smart convenience equals data exchange.
Default settings favor data sharing.
Password discipline reduces risk.
Network segmentation improves security.

What You Should Do Next

Review all connected devices in your home.
Change default passwords.
Audit app permissions.
Update router firmware.

Professional Disclaimer: Cybersecurity threats evolve rapidly. Readers should consult trusted technology professionals for advanced network protection.

Chapter 18

Backup Discipline & Digital Hygiene

If It Exists in One Place, It Is Not Safe

Photos.
Financial records.
Tax returns.
Legal documents.

If stored in one location only — they are vulnerable.

Part I – Cloud Is Not Enough: Cloud storage is convenient, but accounts can be:

Hacked
Locked
Corrupted
Deleted

Maintain at least one additional backup.

Part II – The 3-2-1 Rule: Maintain:

3 copies of important data
2 different storage formats
1 offsite backup

Example:

Primary computer
External hard drive
Cloud storage

Part III – Ransomware Awareness: Never--

Open unknown email attachments
Click unexpected links
Download from unverified sites

One careless click can encrypt an entire system.

Key Takeaways

Single-location storage is risky.
Redundancy equals resilience.
Discipline prevents disaster.

What You Should Do Next

Purchase an external backup drive.
Schedule automatic backups.
Test restore functionality periodically.
Store a copy offsite.

Chapter 19

How Advertising Manipulates You

Emotional Engineering in the Digital Age: Modern advertising is rarely informational. It is psychological.

Common Manipulation Techniques
Scarcity ("Only 12 left")
Authority ("Stanford confirms")
Testimonials without data
Urgency timers
Long-form emotional storytelling
These techniques bypass analytical thinking.

The Pause Rule – Before purchasing:
Wait 24 hours.
Research independent sources.
Ask: "What is the business model?"
Ask: "Who benefits most?"
Impulse benefits sellers. Reflection benefits buyers.

Key Takeaways
Urgency is engineered.
Authority claims require verification.
Emotion is often the entry point.
Waiting reduces regret.

What You Should Do Next
Apply the 24-hour rule to non-essential purchases.
Verify credentials independently.
Avoid products that require immediate action.
Teach these principles to family members.

PART V

Ethics, Leadership & Stewardship

Chapter 20

Character Still Matters

When No One Is Watching – Systems are important. Policies are necessary. Regulations are helpful. But none of them substitute for character.

Over the years, I have worked within industries that rely heavily on disclosure, compliance, and documentation. These are essential. Yet no form, no statute, and no oversight mechanism can fully compensate for the absence of integrity.

Integrity is not complicated. It is doing what is right when it is inconvenient. It is honoring commitments when profit tempts otherwise. It is telling the truth even when the truth reduces immediate gain.

In recent years, I have observed a growing tolerance for shortcuts. Exaggeration is reframed as marketing. Omission is reframed as strategy. Aggressive behavior is reframed as competitiveness. But the consequences remain the same. Families suffer when advisors mislead. Communities weaken when leaders rationalize. Trust erodes quietly — and rebuilding it takes years. Character does not eliminate risk. It reduces avoidable harm.

Practical Implications
Verify before promoting.
Disclose fully before selling.
Document clearly before disputing.

Pause before reacting.
Personal discipline precedes public credibility.

Key Takeaways
Integrity is foundational, not optional.
Short-term gain often creates long-term instability.
Character builds resilience in uncertain environments.

Chapter 21

Compassion Without Naivety: Helping Wisely

Compassion is essential. But compassion without boundaries can create dependency, financial strain, and unintended harm. Many families face difficult choices:

Supporting aging parents
Assisting adult children
Covering medical expenses
Co-signing obligations

Generosity is admirable. Indiscriminate exposure is not.

Helping wisely means:

Understanding your own financial limits
Protecting retirement stability
Avoiding co-signing without clear exit strategies
Ensuring that assistance does not undermine your own long-term care planning

Compassion should strengthen families — not destabilize them.

Practical Framework – Before providing financial assistance:

Can I afford this without jeopardizing retirement security?
Is this a one-time support or an ongoing obligation?
Have expectations been clearly discussed?
Is this enabling avoidable behavior?
Boundaries protect relationships.

Key Takeaways

Compassion requires wisdom.
Financial boundaries preserve dignity.

Helping responsibly protects both parties.

Chapter 22

Stewardship and Preparation

Planning Is Responsibility, Not Fear. Preparation is often misunderstood as pessimism. It is not. Preparation is stewardship. It reflects respect:

For the future
For family
For health
For earned assets

Insurance planning, Social Security analysis, trust structuring, digital discipline — none of these are acts of fear. They are acts of responsibility. Life includes uncertainty. Planning does not eliminate uncertainty. It narrows the damage uncertainty can cause. Stewardship requires:

Honest assessment
Disciplined action
Periodic review
Willingness to adapt

It also requires humility — acknowledging that none of us are immune to error, urgency, or misplaced trust. Preparation is not dramatic. It is steady. And steadiness produces peace.

Final Reflection: This guide has not promised shortcuts. It has not offered miracles. It has not encouraged fear. It has offered structure.

If you carry forward only one principle, let it be this:
Slow down.
Verify.
Document.
Plan.

Order nurtures peace. Peace protects families

Part VI

A Section for Tweens and Teens

A Note to Adults Who Care for Teens and Tweens

This section is directed specifically to our young charges, the teens and tweens who are in the process of exploring and learning our wider world. It is virtually impossible to protect them from everything. I hope that these bits of commentary and suggestions will help them make wise choices.

Chapter 23

Smoking and Vaping

Smoking and Vaping — What's the Real Deal?

Okay, so a lot of people think vaping is "just steam" or that smoking is something adults do, but here's the straight truth: **neither is safe, especially for teens.**

Your Brain Is Still Growing

Your brain keeps developing *until about age 25.* Nicotine — the stuff in cigarettes and most vapes — actually changes how your brain works while it's still growing. That means things like focus, learning stuff, controlling your mood, and thinking straight can all get messed up if you start smoking or vaping early. It doesn't matter if it's a cigarette or a vape — nicotine still affects your brain.

Vaping Isn't Harmless

Vapes might not have all the chemicals that cigarettes do, but they still have **nicotine and other harmful stuff** like heavy metals and chemicals that can hurt your lungs and body. Some flavors might smell sweet, but inhaling them into your lungs is not the same as eating candy.

Addiction Happens Fast

Your brain is especially good at learning new things right now — that's great for school and sports — but it also means it can learn addiction quickly. Nicotine sticks to your brain's reward system, and that can make you *want more* just to feel normal. That's literally what addiction is.

📉 Risks Don't End With "Just Trying"

Some studies show teens who vape are *more likely* to try regular cigarettes later — even if they started vaping because they thought it was "safer." And vaping can still cause coughs, breathing issues, and other health problems.

📊 The Bottom Line

- Smoking and vaping can hurt your brain and lungs.
- Nicotine is addictive and sticks with you.
- Even "just trying" can lead to real problems later.
- Younger brains are *more vulnerable* to lasting harm.
- Choosing not to start protects your health and your future.

Chapter 24

Illegal Drugs and Misusing Medicine: What They Don't Tell You

So here's something most adults don't explain clearly: **you don't have to be using "street drugs" to damage your health.** Even regular medicines can hurt you if they're used the wrong way.

And yes — teens are especially at risk.

🚫 Illegal Drugs: Not Just "Trying It Once"

Illegal drugs like cocaine, meth, heroin, or non-medical marijuana use might look "normal" on social media or in music, but they can seriously change how your brain works.

Your brain is still wiring itself for decision-making and self-control. Drugs interfere with that wiring. Some drugs flood your brain with dopamine (the "feel good" chemical). That might sound nice, but when your brain gets overloaded, it can stop producing normal amounts on its own. That's how addiction starts.[1]

Some drugs can also:

- Damage memory and learning
- Increase anxiety or depression
- Raise risk of psychosis (losing touch with reality)
- Increase risk of overdose

And overdose isn't rare. Synthetic opioids like fentanyl are now involved in many teen overdose deaths because they're mixed into other drugs without people knowing.

Prescription Drugs — Safe When Used Correctly, Dangerous When Not

This part surprises a lot of people.

Prescription medicines are safe **when taken exactly as prescribed by a doctor for the right person**.

But taking:

- Someone else's ADHD medication
- Extra pain pills
- Anxiety meds not prescribed to you
- Sleep medications "for fun"

—that's drug misuse.

Commonly misused prescription drugs include:[3]

- **Opioids** (pain pills)
- **Stimulants** (ADHD meds like amphetamines)
- **Benzodiazepines** (anxiety meds)

Misusing them can cause:

- Slowed breathing
- Irregular heartbeat
- Seizures
- Coma
- Death

And mixing them (especially opioids with alcohol or benzodiazepines) is extremely dangerous.

Over-the-Counter (OTC) Doesn't Mean Harmless

Even cough medicine can be abused. Some teens misuse products containing dextromethorphan (DXM) to get high.[4]

Large amounts can cause:

- Hallucinations
- Vomiting
- Brain damage
- Dangerous heart rhythm problems

OTC medicines are designed for specific doses. Taking more does not make them work better. It just makes them risky.

Why Teens Are More Vulnerable

The teenage brain:

- Is more sensitive to rewards
- Has not fully developed impulse control
- Is still forming long-term judgment skills

That makes addiction easier and faster in teens compared to adults.[1]

What feels like "just experimenting" can change brain pathways in ways that are hard to undo.

The Bottom Line

- Illegal drugs can permanently change your brain.
- Prescription drugs are not safe unless used exactly as prescribed for you.
- OTC medicine can be dangerous in high doses.
- Addiction happens faster in teens.
- One bad decision can have permanent consequences.

Being smart now protects your freedom later.

Chapter 25

Screen Time & Mobile Devices: Who's Really in Control?

📱 Screen Time and Mobile Devices — Who's Really in Control?

Let's be honest.

Most of us don't even remember life without a phone. It's our alarm clock, music player, camera, social life, homework helper — everything.

But here's the real question:

Are we using our phones... or are they using us?

🧠 Your Brain on Screens

Apps are designed to keep you scrolling. Notifications, likes, streaks — they trigger dopamine, the same brain chemical involved in reward and addiction.

Your brain is still developing its self-control system. That part (the prefrontal cortex) doesn't fully mature until your mid-20s. So constant digital stimulation can make it harder to:

- Focus
- Be patient
- Delay gratification
- Sleep well

It's not about being "weak." It's about brain science.

😴 Sleep Gets Hit First

Blue light from screens can delay melatonin, the hormone that tells your body it's time to sleep.[2]

Teens already need about 8–10 hours of sleep per night.[3] But scrolling at midnight makes that almost impossible.

Lack of sleep can lead to:

- Mood swings
- Lower grades
- Weaker immune system
- Higher risk of anxiety and depression

And when you're tired, your decision-making drops.

😟 Mental Health and Comparison Culture

Social media can connect people — but it also creates constant comparison. Seeing filtered lives all day can make you feel:

- Not good enough
- Behind
- Less attractive
- Less successful

Research shows heavy social media use in teens is linked to higher rates of anxiety and depressive symptoms. It doesn't mean social media is evil. It means too much exposure without boundaries can affect mental health.

👀 Attention and Focus

If you switch between homework and your phone every few minutes, your brain has to keep "reloading" tasks. Studies show multitasking actually lowers efficiency and memory retention. So when you feel like you studied for hours but don't remember much — that might be why.

⚖️ It's Not About Throwing Your Phone Away

Technology isn't the enemy. It's powerful. It helps us learn, connect, create, and grow. The key is **balance and boundaries**:

- Keep devices out of your bedroom at night.
- Turn off non-essential notifications.
- Set app time limits.
- Take "no-phone" breaks during the day.
- Spend time face-to-face with real people.

The goal isn't perfection. The goal is being in control.

💬 The Bottom Line

- Your brain is still developing and sensitive to constant stimulation.
- Too much screen time affects sleep and mood.
- Social media comparison can harm self-confidence.
- Multitasking reduces focus and memory.
- Smart boundaries protect your mental health.

Your phone should be a tool — not your boss.

Chapter 26

Diet, Spending Habits, & How Early Choices Shape Your Future

Food Choices, Money Choices — Small Habits, Big Consequences

Let's be real: Nobody wakes up at 14 thinking, "Today I will damage my future." But small everyday choices — what we eat and how we spend money — quietly build our future one decision at a time.

Diet: You Can't Run a High-Performance Brain on Junk Fuel

Your body is still growing. Your brain is still wiring itself. That means what you eat actually matters more now than later.

A steady diet of:

- Soda
- Energy drinks
- Candy
- Fast food
- Ultra-processed snacks

can lead to:

- Weight gain
- Fatigue
- Mood swings
- Poor concentration
- Increased risk of type 2 diabetes

Teens who regularly consume high amounts of added sugar and ultra-processed foods have higher risks of obesity and metabolic problems. And here's something most people don't say clearly:

Food affects your mood.

Diets high in processed foods are associated with higher rates of depressive symptoms in adolescents. That doesn't mean you can't have pizza. It means pizza shouldn't be your main food group.

Simple Upgrades That Actually Work

- Drink water most of the time.
- Eat protein (eggs, chicken, beans, nuts).
- Add fruits and vegetables daily.
- Don't skip breakfast.

The Mediterranean-style eating pattern — lots of vegetables, whole grains, healthy fats, lean protein — is linked to better long-term heart and brain health.

You don't need perfection. You need consistency.

Misusing Pocket Money — Practice for the Future

Allowance, birthday cash, part-time job money — this is training ground money.

If every dollar goes to:

- Fast food
- Game add-ons
- Trendy items
- Impulse buys

then you're practicing short-term thinking. Financial habits formed in adolescence often continue into adulthood. Spending without thinking trains your brain to chase quick rewards instead of long-term goals.

Delayed Gratification = Power

One of the strongest predictors of future success is the ability to delay gratification — choosing something better later instead of something small now.[5]

Saving even a small percentage of your money builds:

- Discipline
- Confidence
- Independence

You don't need a lot of money to build the habit.

You just need the decision.

The Bottom Line

- Your body and brain need real fuel.
- Too much sugar and processed food affects mood and health.
- Money habits start early.
- Spending wisely builds independence.
- Small consistent choices beat big dramatic changes.

Your future self is being built right now — one snack and one dollar at a time.

Chapter 27

Developing Good Habits Early – Building a Life You're Proud Of

Here's something adults don't always say clearly: You don't suddenly "become responsible" at 25. You build responsibility one habit at a time.

Right now.

Habits Shape Your Brain

Your brain is especially flexible during your teen years. Scientists call this **neuroplasticity** — your brain is constantly wiring and rewiring based on what you repeat. That means:

- The habits you practice now get stronger.
- The behaviors you repeat become automatic.
- The patterns you build become your "normal."

Good habits feel small at first; but repeated daily, they become powerful.

Discipline Is Freedom (Not Punishment)

Waking up on time. Finishing homework before scrolling. Practicing a skill consistently. Saving part of your money. Those aren't "boring adult rules." They're training for independence.

Research shows that self-control in adolescence is strongly linked to better physical health, financial stability, and fewer legal problems in adulthood.[2]

In other words: discipline today equals options tomorrow.

Physical Habits Matter Too

Regular exercise improves:

- Mood
- Sleep
- Memory
- Confidence

The Centers for Disease Control and Prevention recommends at least 60 minutes of physical activity per day for teens. That doesn't mean gym membership. It can be walking, sports, dancing, pushups in your room — just move. Movement strengthens your body and your brain.

Reading and Learning Build Real Confidence

Scrolling gives information. Reading builds understanding.

Teens who read regularly develop stronger vocabulary, better com-prehension, and improved critical thinking skills.

When you understand more, you feel more capable. And confidence built on skill is solid — not fake.

Choose Your Circle Carefully

You become more like the people you spend time with.

Peer influence during adolescence is powerful because your brain is highly responsive to social belonging.[5]

If your friends:

- Skip class
- Use substances
- Mock effort
- Live for drama —you'll feel pressure to match that energy.

If your friends:

- Work toward goals
- Respect others
- Take care of themselves —that rubs off too. Choose wisely.

Small Daily Wins Add Up

Good habits are not dramatic. They are:

- Making your bed.
- Showing up on time.
- Being honest.
- Keeping your word.
- Taking care of your health.

No one applauds these daily, but they build character; and character lasts longer than trends.

The Bottom Line

- Your brain is building itself right now.
- Repeated behaviors become automatic habits.
- Discipline increases freedom and options.
- Movement, reading, and strong friendships matter.
- Small consistent actions shape your future.

You don't need to be perfect.

You just need to practice becoming the person you want to be.

Every day counts.

Conclusion

This is Just the Tip of the Iceberg; Order in the Chaos – And in Your Life

Not long ago, I stood in the middle of my childhood home surrounded by boxes. Some held memories. Others held evidence of decisions I wish I had made differently — supplements that promised more than they delivered, policies I had let lapse, products I had purchased in moments of urgency rather than reflection.

I did not write this book from a place of having it all figured out. I wrote it from a place of having learned — sometimes painfully — what happens when urgency replaces discernment, when hope substitutes for planning, and when the noise of the world drowns out the quiet discipline that good decisions require. That is the thread that runs through every chapter of this guide.

When I counsel clients about long-term care, I am not just reciting statistics. I am thinking about the moment I realized that the policy I had faithfully paid for — and then surrendered in a difficult season — could not be replaced at any reasonable cost. I am thinking about the families who call me after a diagnosis, asking what can be done now, and having to tell them that the window for easy options has closed.

When I write about Social Security strategy, I am thinking about the widow who discovered, too late, that her husband's early claiming decision had permanently reduced the income she would live on for the rest of her life.

When I address health misinformation and supplement hype, I am thinking about my own boxes, my own hope, my own monthly charges for things that sounded promising and cost me more than money.

And when I speak to our young people in Part VI, I am thinking about the world they are inheriting — noisier, faster, and more manipulative than the one I entered. I want them to have tools I did not have at their age. I want them to slow down before society, peers, and culture teach and pressure them to speed up.

If this book has done its work, you are leaving it with more than information. You are leaving it with a framework — a way of pausing before acting, questioning before accepting, and planning before the crisis arrives.

The world will continue to accelerate. Advertisements will grow more sophisticated. Offers will become more urgent. The line between professional guidance and persuasive marketing will continue to blur. None of that is likely to change. What can change is how you respond to it.

You do not need to be suspicious of everything. You do not need to be paralyzed by complexity. You need only to slow down enough to ask the right questions:

- Who benefits from this decision?
- What am I being asked to act on — and why now?
- Have I verified this, or am I responding to urgency?
- Does this align with my long-term stability, or only my immediate comfort?

Those four questions, applied consistently, will protect you more reliably than any single product, policy, or promise ever could.

I am not finished learning, nor making mistakes. I am still navigating the same world you are — with medical realities, financial pressures, digital noise, and the daily challenge of choosing wisely when everything around me is designed to make me choose quickly. But I have learned this much: order is possible. Not the absence of chaos — that is not realistic; but a personal discipline, a steady practice of discernment, that creates peace in the middle of chaos.

Order nurtures peace. Peace produces stability. Stability protects families. That has been true in every chapter of this book. It is true in every chapter of a life well-considered.

Thank you for reading. Now, go make a plan.

— Andrea Hoxie.

Appendices

Glossary of Key Terms

Decision Ladders (Collected)

Checklists

Resource Indices

Trusted Service Providers

Disclaimers

Glossary of Key Terms

Terms are listed alphabetically within each topic category. Chapter references are noted in brackets where applicable.

This glossary is intended as a quick reference. For full context, refer to the chapter in which each term appears.

Long-Term Care & Insurance (Chapters 1–2)

Activities of Daily Living (ADLs) *[Ch. 1–2]*

Basic self-care tasks — including bathing, dressing, eating, toileting, transferring (moving from bed to chair), and continence — used by insurers to determine when long-term care benefits are triggered. Most policies require the inability to perform two or more ADLs.

Asset Repositioning *[Ch. 2]*

A strategy in which existing assets (such as a savings account, CD, or life insurance policy) are transferred or exchanged to fund a hybrid long-term care product. Rather than paying new premiums from income, the policyholder redirects assets already owned.

Benefit Pool *[Ch. 2]*

The total dollar amount available under a long-term care insurance policy. Once the pool is exhausted, benefits end. For example, a policy with a $300,000 benefit pool paying $5,000 per month would last approximately 60 months if fully utilized.

Benefit Trigger *[Ch. 1–2]*

The qualifying condition that must be met before a long-term care insurance policy begins paying benefits. Most policies use two standards: inability to perform two or more Activities of Daily Living (ADLs), or a diagnosis of cognitive impairment such as dementia.

Elimination Period *[Ch. 2]*

The waiting period between the start of a qualifying care need and the first day that insurance benefits are paid — similar to a deductible measured in time rather than dollars. Common elimination periods are 30, 60, or 90 days. The policyholder is responsible for care costs during this period.

Hybrid / Asset-Based LTC Policy *[Ch. 2]*

A life insurance policy or annuity that includes a long-term care rider. If the insured requires long-term care, benefits are accelerated from the death benefit. If care is never needed, a death benefit passes to heirs. Premiums are typically guaranteed not to increase.

Indemnity Coverage *[Ch. 1]*

A type of insurance benefit structure in which the policy pays a fixed daily or monthly amount regardless of actual care costs incurred — as opposed to a reimbursement model, which pays only for documented expenses up to the benefit limit.

Inflation Rider *[Ch. 2]*

An optional addition to a long-term care policy that increases the benefit amount over time — typically by a fixed percentage (e.g., 3% or 5% annually) — to help keep pace with rising care costs. Without an inflation rider, a policy purchased today may cover significantly less care in 20 years.

Leverage Ratio (LTC context) *[Ch. 2]*

The relationship between premiums paid and the total benefit available under a long-term care policy. A high leverage ratio means a relatively small premium buys a large benefit pool — generally more favorable in traditional LTC policies than hybrid products.

Medicaid Five-Year Lookback *[Ch. 1]*

A Medicaid rule that examines financial transactions made in the five years prior to a long-term care Medicaid application. Asset transfers made for less than fair market value during this period can result in a penalty — a period during which Medicaid will not cover care costs.

Reimbursement Model *[Ch. 2]*

An insurance benefit structure in which the policy pays only for documented, qualifying care expenses — up to the daily or monthly benefit limit. The insured must submit receipts or invoices; unused daily benefits may or may not carry over, depending on the policy.

Self-Insure *[Ch. 1]*

A financial strategy in which an individual accepts the full risk of a potential expense — such as long-term care costs — by setting aside personal assets rather than purchasing insurance. Appropriate only when assets are sufficient to absorb potentially large, prolonged expenses.

Underwriting *[Ch. 1-2]*

The process by which an insurance company evaluates an applicant's health history, age, and risk factors to determine eligibility for coverage and set premium rates. Medical underwriting becomes more restrictive as applicants age or develop health conditions — making early application advantageous.

Medicare (Chapter 2 — Medicare Basics)

Formulary *[Ch. 2]*

The list of prescription drugs covered under a Medicare Part D drug plan or Medicare Advantage plan. Each plan maintains its own formulary, organized into cost tiers. A drug not on a plan's formulary may require prior authorization or step therapy before coverage is approved.

IRMAA (Income-Related Monthly Adjustment Amount) *[Ch. 2]*

A surcharge added to Medicare Part B and Part D premiums for beneficiaries whose income exceeds certain thresholds. IRMAA is based on income reported two years prior. Higher earners may pay significantly more than the standard Medicare premium.

Medicare Advantage (Part C) *[Ch. 2]*

An alternative to Original Medicare offered by private insurers. Plans must cover all Original Medicare benefits and typically include prescription drug coverage. They often feature lower premiums but may restrict provider networks and require prior authorizations.

Medicare Part A *[Ch. 2]*

The hospital insurance component of Original Medicare, covering inpatient hospital stays, skilled nursing facility care (under specific conditions), hospice, and some home health services. Most beneficiaries pay no premium for Part A if they or their spouse paid Medicare taxes for at least 10 years.

Medicare Part B *[Ch. 2]*

The medical insurance component of Original Medicare, covering outpatient care, physician services, preventive care, and durable medical equipment. Part B requires a monthly premium.

Medicare Part D *[Ch. 2]*

Prescription drug coverage under Medicare, offered through private insurers. Part D plans vary in premiums, deductibles, and formularies. Enrollment during the Initial Enrollment Period is important — late enrollment penalties apply and accumulate permanently.

Medicare Supplement (Medigap) *[Ch. 2]*

A private insurance policy that works alongside Original Medicare (Parts A and B) to cover cost-sharing gaps such as deductibles, copayments, and coinsurance. Medigap plans are standardized by letter (e.g., Plan G, Plan N). Federal law prohibits holding more than one Medigap policy simultaneously.

Open Enrollment Period (OEP) *[Ch. 2]*

A defined window during which individuals may enroll in, switch, or drop Medicare plans without medical underwriting or penalty. The Annual Medicare Open Enrollment Period runs October 15 through December 7 each year.

Pharmacy Benefit Manager (PBM) *[Ch. 2–3]*

A third-party administrator that manages prescription drug benefits on behalf of insurers, Medicare plans, and employers. PBMs negotiate drug prices, maintain formularies, and process pharmacy claims. Major PBMs include OptumRx, CVS Caremark, and Express Scripts — often subsidiaries of vertically integrated healthcare companies.

Prior Authorization *[Ch. 2]*

A requirement imposed by an insurer or Medicare Advantage plan that a provider obtain approval before a service, procedure, or prescription is covered. Failure to obtain prior authorization can result in denied claims. Patients have the right to appeal denials.

Special Enrollment Period (SEP) *[Ch. 2, 8]*

A window outside of standard enrollment periods during which individuals may enroll in or change Medicare or ACA marketplace coverage due to qualifying life events — such as losing employer coverage, moving, or gaining or losing Medicaid eligibility.

Financial Planning, Legal & Estate Terms (Chapters 7-11)

ACA Premium Tax Credit *[Ch. 8]*

A federal subsidy available to individuals and families who purchase health insurance through the ACA marketplace and whose household income falls within eligible thresholds. The credit reduces monthly premium costs and is calculated based on income relative to the Federal Poverty Level.

Beneficiary *[Ch. 9]*

A person or entity designated to receive assets or benefits upon the death of the policyholder, account holder, or trust grantor. Beneficiary designations on insurance policies, retirement accounts, and payable-on-death accounts typically override instructions in a will.

Estate Planning *[Ch. 9]*

The process of arranging for the management and distribution of one's assets during life and after death. A complete estate plan typically includes a will, powers of attorney, healthcare directives, beneficiary designations, and possibly trust structures.

Fiduciary *[Ch. 11]*

A person or institution legally and ethically obligated to act in the best interest of another party. A fiduciary financial advisor must prioritize the client's interests over their own — a higher standard than the suitability standard applied to some brokers and salespeople.

FINRA (Financial Industry Regulatory Authority) *[Ch. 11]*

A nonprofit self-regulatory organization that oversees broker-dealers and investment advisors in the United States. FINRA's BrokerCheck tool (brokercheck.finra.org) allows consumers to verify the registration status and disciplinary history of financial professionals.

Full Retirement Age (FRA) *[Ch. 7]*

The age at which a Social Security beneficiary is entitled to receive 100% of their calculated benefit. FRA varies by birth year — for those born in 1960 or later, FRA is 67. Claiming before FRA permanently reduces monthly benefits; delaying past FRA increases them up to age 70.

Irrevocable Trust *[Ch. 9]*

A trust that, once established, cannot generally be modified or revoked without the consent of its beneficiaries. Assets transferred into an irrevocable trust are typically removed from the grantor's taxable estate and may offer protection from creditors and Medicaid spend-down — but at the cost of control.

Probate *[Ch. 9]*

The legal process by which a deceased person's estate is administered under court supervision — validating the will, paying debts, and distributing assets. Probate can be time-consuming and costly. Assets held in trusts or with named beneficiaries typically bypass probate.

Reasonable Compensation (S Corp) *[Ch. 10]*

The IRS requirement that S Corporation owner-employees pay themselves a salary comparable to what the market would pay for similar services. Failure to pay reasonable compensation — and instead taking all income as distributions to avoid payroll taxes — is a common audit trigger.

Revocable Living Trust *[Ch. 9]*

A trust created during the grantor's lifetime that can be modified or revoked at any time. Assets held in a revocable trust typically avoid probate but remain part of the grantor's taxable estate and are not protected from Medicaid spend-down or creditors.

S Corporation (S Corp) *[Ch. 10]*

A business structure that passes income, losses, deductions, and credits through to shareholders for federal tax purposes, avoiding corporate-level taxation. S Corps can offer tax advantages related to self-employment taxes but involve specific IRS rules — including requirements for reasonable compensation.

Social Security Earnings Test *[Ch. 7]*

An IRS rule that reduces Social Security benefits for individuals who claim before Full Retirement Age and continue to work and earn above a threshold amount. Once FRA is reached, the earnings test no longer applies and previously withheld benefits are recalculated.

Spend-Down *[Ch. 1, 9]*

The process of reducing personal assets to qualify for Medicaid long-term care coverage. Medicaid has strict asset and income limits; individuals with assets above those limits must exhaust resources — through care costs or allowable transfers — before Medicaid coverage begins.

Consumer Protection, Digital Safety & Media Literacy (Chapters 12–18)

Data Breach *[Ch. 16–17]*

An incident in which unauthorized individuals gain access to private, protected, or sensitive information — such as names, Social Security numbers, financial account data, or medical records. Consumers affected by a data breach should monitor credit reports and consider placing a credit freeze.

Demand Letter *[Ch. 12]*

A formal written notice sent to an individual, business, or institution demanding specific action — such as a refund, correction, or cessation of a practice — within a stated timeframe, and typically warning of legal or regulatory action if the demand is not met.

Dopamine Loop *[Ch. 24]*

A behavioral pattern in which variable rewards — such as likes, notifications, or new content — trigger repeated dopamine releases in the brain, reinforcing continued engagement. App and social media designers intentionally leverage this mechanism to increase user time on platform.

Phishing *[Ch. 15–16]*

A fraudulent attempt — typically via email, text, or phone — to trick individuals into revealing sensitive information such as passwords, account numbers, or Social Security numbers, usually by impersonating a legitimate institution.

Robocall *[Ch. 15]*

An automated phone call that delivers a pre-recorded message, often used in telemarketing, scams, or political campaigns. The FCC requires legitimate robocallers to obtain prior consent. Unwanted robocalls can be reported to the FTC at reportfraud.ftc.gov.

Spoofing *[Ch. 15]*

The practice of falsifying the caller ID, email address, or website URL displayed to a recipient in order to appear as a trusted source — such as a government agency, bank, or local number. Spoofed calls are a common tool in phone-based fraud schemes.

Two-Factor Authentication (2FA) *[Ch. 16–17]*

A security process that requires two forms of verification to access an account — typically a password plus a one-time code sent via text or generated by an app. Two-factor authentication significantly reduces the risk of unauthorized account access even if a password is compromised.

VPN (Virtual Private Network) *[Ch. 16]*

A service that encrypts internet traffic and masks a user's IP address, reducing the ability of third parties — such as advertisers, hackers on public Wi-Fi, or internet service providers — to monitor online activity. VPN use is recommended when connecting to public or unsecured networks.

Health, Science & Media Terms (Chapters 4–6, 22–26)

Anecdotal Evidence *[Ch. 4–6]*

A personal story or individual account used to support a claim. Anecdotal evidence is not a substitute for controlled scientific research. Testimonials in supplement or health product advertising are a common form of anecdotal evidence and are not proof of efficacy.

Cognitive Impairment *[Ch. 1–2]*

A decline in mental functions — including memory, reasoning, language, or judgment — beyond what is expected with normal aging. Cognitive impairment (including Alzheimer's disease and other dementias) is one of the two primary benefit triggers recognized by long-term care insurance policies.

Delayed Gratification *[Ch. 25]*

The ability to resist an immediate reward in favor of a larger or more valuable reward in the future. Research identifies delayed gratification as a strong predictor of long-term financial stability, academic success, and overall life outcomes.

Neuroplasticity *[Ch. 26]*

The brain's ability to reorganize itself by forming new neural connections throughout life — especially during adolescence. Neuroplasticity means that habits, learning, and repeated behaviors during the teen years can have lasting effects on brain development and automatic behavior patterns.

Placebo Effect *[Ch. 4]*

The measurable improvement in a patient's condition resulting from a treatment that has no active pharmacological ingredient — driven by expectation and belief. The placebo effect is why controlled clinical trials compare treatments against placebos rather than no treatment at all.

Pulmonary Sarcoidosis *[Ch. 1]*

An inflammatory disease that causes small clusters of cells (granulomas) to form in the lungs and other organs. Sarcoidosis can range from mild to severe; some cases resolve on their own while others require treatment. Referenced in the author's personal account in Chapter 1.

Randomized Controlled Trial (RCT) *[Ch. 4–5]*

A scientific study design in which participants are randomly assigned to receive either a treatment or a placebo (or comparison treatment). RCTs are considered the gold standard for evaluating whether a supplement, drug, or intervention actually causes an effect.

Vertical Integration (Healthcare) *[Ch. 3]*

A business structure in which a single corporate entity controls multiple stages of the healthcare supply chain — such as hospitals, physician practices, insurance plans, and pharmacy benefit managers. Vertical integration can reduce competition and complicate consumer advocacy.

All definitions are provided for general educational purposes only. Legal, financial, insurance, and medical terms may carry specific meanings under applicable law, regulation, or policy contract language that differ from these plain-language explanations. Consult qualified professionals for guidance specific to your situation.

Decision Ladders

ESTATE PLANNING DECISION LADDER

A Broad Overview — Protecting What You've Built & the People You Love

▼ START HERE ▼

Have you taken steps to protect your assets and your loved ones?

↓

1 BASIC DOCS

Do you have a Will?

YES → **Review & Update It**
Marriage, divorce, birth, or death require updates. [*Consult an estate attorney*]

NO → **Create a Last Will & Testament**
Without one, the state decides who gets what. [*Consult an estate attorney*]

2 TRUST

Do you want to avoid probate or protect privacy?

YES → **Revocable Living Trust**
Assets transfer privately, bypassing probate court. [*Consult an estate attorney*]

NO → A will alone may suffice — ensure all beneficiaries are current.

3 POA & HEALTH

Who speaks for you if you cannot?

FIN. → **Durable Power of Attorney**
Authorizes someone to manage your finances.

MED. → **Healthcare POA + Living Will / Advance Directive**
Directs medical care & end-of-life decisions. [*Consult an attorney & your physician*]

4 BENE-FICI-ARIES

Are your beneficiaries & accounts properly titled?

YES → Review every 3–5 years or after any major life event.

NO → **Update Beneficiaries on All Accounts**
Life insurance, retirement, bank & investment accounts.
[*Outdated designations override your will*]

5 TAX & LEGACY

Consider Tax Strategy & Legacy Giving
Estate taxes, gifting strategies, charitable trusts, & life insurance as a wealth-transfer tool can preserve more for your heirs. [*Consult an estate attorney & financial advisor*]

Grand Pea, Inc. | *grandpeainsurance.com* | *For educational purposes only. Work with a licensed attorney, financial advisor, and insurance professional for personalized guidance.*

BEFORE YOU DECIDE

A Decision Ladder for Real Life — Because Every Choice Has a Next Step

You're going to face hard choices. That's real life. This ladder isn't here to lecture you — it's here to help you think it through *before* you act, so you stay in control of your own story.

▼ SOMETHING FEELS OFF — PAUSE HERE ▼

Are you being pressured — or tempted — to do something that doesn't feel right?

↓

GUT CHECK

Would you be okay if someone you respect saw you do this?

YES → Still think it through — but you're probably on solid ground. *Keep going ↓*

NO → **That feeling is data. Trust it.**
Your gut is telling you something important — listen. *Slow down ↓*

CONSEQUENCES

Could this hurt you, someone else, or your future?

YES → **Think about: your health, your record, your reputation, your relationships.**
Substances, risky behavior, and bad decisions leave real marks. *This is a stop sign.*

NO → Good. Keep thinking it through. *Keep going ↓*

PEER PRESSURE

Are you doing this because YOU want to — or because someone else wants you to?

THEM → **Real friends don't require you to risk yourself to fit in.**
It's okay to say: "That's not for me." Full stop. *You don't owe anyone a yes.*

ME → Own your choice — and own what comes with it. *Keep going ↓*

EXIT PLAN

Do you have a safe way out if things go wrong?

YES → Good. Know your exit before you walk in. *You're thinking smart.*

NO → **Set one up first.**
Code word with a trusted adult, a friend who knows where you are, a way to leave.
Tell someone you trust where you'll be.

STILL UNSURE?

Talk to someone you trust — before you act.
A parent, counselor, mentor, coach, or trusted adult. If you're in danger right now: call or text 988 (Crisis Lifeline) or text HOME to 741741 (Crisis Text Line). You are worth protecting.
Asking for help is strength, not weakness.

Checklists

IN CASE OF EMERGENCY

Critical Information Others Need to Know — Fill In & Keep Accessible

Complete this page and share it with at least one trusted person. Keep a copy in your home, your wallet, and with your important documents.

ABOUT ME

Full Legal Name

Date of Birth　　Blood Type

Home Address

Cell Phone

Social Security # (last 4 only)

EMERGENCY CONTACTS

Contact 1 — Name & Relationship

Phone

Contact 2 — Name & Relationship

Phone

Attorney — Name & Phone

Financial Advisor — Name & Phone

Insurance Agent — Name & Phone

MEDICAL — PRIMARY CARE

Primary Care Physician

Phone

Preferred Hospital

MEDICATIONS & ALLERGIES

Current Medications (list or attach)

Known Allergies (medications, foods, other)

Major Medical Conditions

KEY DOCUMENTS — LOCATION

Will / Trust

Power of Attorney

Advance Directive / Living Will

Life Insurance Policy / Company

Health Insurance — Company & ID #

Medicare / Medicaid # (if applicable)

ACCESS & ACCOUNTS

Primary Bank & Account #

Safe / Safe Deposit Box Location

Password Manager / Digital Access Info

Store passwords securely — not on this sheet.

Grand Pea, Inc. | *grandpeainsurance.com* | *Keep this document in a secure but accessible location. Review and update annually or after any major life change.*

PERSONAL PLANNING DOCUMENTS

A Checklist — Do You Have What You Need?

Having the right documents in place — and knowing where they are — protects you and the people you love. Check off what you have, and make a plan to get what you don't.

LEGAL DOCUMENTS

- ☐ **Last Will & Testament** *Signed, witnessed, notarized*
- ☐ **Revocable Living Trust** *If applicable*
- ☐ **Durable Power of Attorney** *Financial decisions*
- ☐ **Healthcare Power of Attorney** *Medical decisions*
- ☐ **Living Will / Advance Directive** *End-of-life wishes*
- ☐ **POLST / DNR Form** *If applicable — keep accessible*
- ☐ **Guardianship Designation** *For minor children*

FINANCIAL DOCUMENTS

- ☐ **Bank & Investment Account List** *With account numbers & institutions*
- ☐ **Retirement Account Statements** *401(k), IRA, pension*
- ☐ **Beneficiary Designations** *Current & on file with each institution*
- ☐ **Property Deeds & Vehicle Titles**
- ☐ **Safe Deposit Box Info** *Location & key*
- ☐ **Digital Assets List** *Online accounts, crypto, passwords*
- ☐ **Social Security Benefit Statement** *Annual SSA estimate*

IDENTITY DOCUMENTS

- ☐ **Birth Certificate**
- ☐ **Social Security Card**
- ☐ **Passport** *Current & not expired*
- ☐ **Driver's License / State ID**
- ☐ **Marriage / Divorce Certificate** *If applicable*
- ☐ **Military Discharge Papers (DD-214)** *If applicable*
- ☐ **Naturalization Certificate** *If applicable*

INSURANCE & BENEFITS

- ☐ **Life Insurance Policies** *Company, policy #, beneficiary*
- ☐ **Health Insurance Cards & Policy**
- ☐ **Medicare / Medicaid Cards** *If applicable*
- ☐ **Long-Term Care Insurance Policy** *If applicable*
- ☐ **Homeowner's / Renter's Policy**

STORAGE & ACCESS

- ☐ **Trusted person knows where documents are**
- ☐ **Copies stored securely** *Fireproof safe or secure cloud*
- ☐ **Attorney has copies of legal docs**

Grand Pea, Inc. | *grandpeainsurance.com* | *For educational purposes only. Consult a licensed attorney and financial advisor for personalized guidance.*

HOW TO READ A SUPPLEMENT LABEL

A Checklist for Smart, Informed Choices

> Not all supplements are created equal. Use this checklist before you buy or take any dietary supplement — your health depends on knowing what's actually in the bottle.

✓ IDENTITY & MANUFACTURER

- ☐ **Product name and intended use are clearly stated** — not vague or overly broad.
- ☐ **Manufacturer name, address, and contact info** are listed on the label.
- ☐ **Third-party verification seal present** (USP, NSF, ConsumerLab, Informed Sport).
  Look for this — it matters.

✓ SUPPLEMENT FACTS PANEL

- ☐ **Serving size and servings per container** are clearly listed.
- ☐ **Each ingredient is named** with its amount per serving (mg, mcg, IU, etc.).
- ☐ **"Proprietary blend"** — individual ingredient amounts are hidden. *Caution: you don't know exact doses.*
- ☐ **% Daily Value (%DV)** is shown where applicable.

✓ INGREDIENTS & ADDITIVES

- ☐ **Other ingredients** (fillers, binders, coatings) are listed — check for allergens.
- ☐ **No artificial dyes, high-risk preservatives, or undisclosed allergens** (gluten, soy, dairy, nuts).
  Red flag if unlisted.
- ☐ **Herb or botanical ingredients** — confirm the plant part used (root, leaf, seed) and extraction ratio are stated.

✓ CLAIMS & WARNINGS

- ☐ **Disease cure claims** ("cures," "treats," "reverses") are illegal for supplements. *Walk away.*
- ☐ **FDA disclaimer present:** "This statement has not been evaluated by the FDA…"
- ☐ **Warnings for pregnancy, nursing, children, or drug interactions** are noted where applicable.
- ☐ **Expiration date and lot number** are printed on the package.

Grand Pea, Inc. | *grandpeainsurance.com* | *For educational purposes only. Always consult your physician or pharmacist before starting any supplement.*

Resources

A consolidated directory of trusted organizations, government agencies, and tools — organized by chapter topic.

PART I — Health & Medical Reality

Chapters 1–2: Long-Term Care Planning

Coverage options, cost data, and counseling for long-term care decisions.

Resource	What It Provides
Genworth Cost of Care Survey www.genworth.com/aging-and-you/finances/cost-of-care.html	Annual national and state-level LTC cost data by care type
AARP Long-Term Care Resources www.aarp.org/caregiving	Guides on LTC options, caregiving planning, and cost tools
ElderLawAnswers www.elderlawanswers.com	Legal and financial planning guides for seniors, including Medicaid
Medicaid.gov — LTSS www.medicaid.gov/medicaid/long-term-services-supports/index.html	Federal Medicaid LTSS eligibility rules, by state
American Association for LTC Insurance www.aaltci.org	Policy comparison, cost benchmarks, and agent locator

Chapter 2: Medicare Basics

Official guidance and free counseling for Medicare options.

Resource	What It Provides
Medicare.gov www.medicare.gov	Official Medicare plan finder, coverage explanations, and enrollment
SHIP — Free Medicare Counseling www.shiphelp.org	Free, unbiased Medicare counseling — local advisors in every state
Medicare Rights Center www.medicarerights.org	Consumer helpline and guides on rights and appeals

Resource	What It Provides
Kaiser Family Foundation Medicare www.kff.org/medicare	Nonpartisan research and explainers on Medicare policy

Chapter 3: Healthcare Vertical Integration

Resource	What It Provides
American Hospital Association www.aha.org	Hospital system data, merger trends, and advocacy resources
Health Affairs Journal www.healthaffairs.org	Peer-reviewed research on healthcare systems and policy
Covering Health (AHCJ) healthjournalism.org	Context on healthcare industry reporting for informed consumers

Chapters 4–5: Supplements & Brain Health

Resource	What It Provides
Examine.com www.examine.com	Independent, evidence-based supplement research database
NIH Office of Dietary Supplements ods.od.nih.gov	Fact sheets and research on vitamins, minerals, and supplements
ConsumerLab.com www.consumerlab.com	Independent testing of supplement quality and label accuracy
NIH — NCCIH www.nccih.nih.gov	Evidence reviews on herbal and alternative health products
Alzheimer's Association www.alz.org	Credible guidance on brain health, cognitive decline, and caregiving

Chapter 6: Spotting Health Misinformation

Resource	What It Provides
NIH MedlinePlus medlineplus.gov	Reliable health information from the National Institutes of Health
Snopes Health www.snopes.com/fact-check/category/health	Fact-checking of widely circulated health stories and claims
CDC www.cdc.gov	Official public health guidance and disease information

PART II — Insurance and Financial Protection

Chapter 7: Social Security Strategy

Resource	What It Provides
SSA.gov — my Social Security www.ssa.gov/myaccount	View earnings record, estimates, and manage benefits online
NARSSA www.narssa.org	Locate a Registered Social Security Analyst for personalized strategy
AARP Social Security Center www.aarp.org/retirement/social-security	Claiming strategies, spousal benefits, and break-even calculators
OpenSocialSecurity.com www.opensocialsecurity.com	Free open-source Social Security optimization calculator

Chapter 8: ACA and Premium Tax Credits

Resource	What It Provides
Healthcare.gov www.healthcare.gov	Official ACA marketplace enrollment and plan comparison
KFF Subsidy Calculator www.kff.org/interactive/subsidy-calculator	Estimate ACA premium tax credits based on income and family size
Benefits.gov www.benefits.gov	Federal eligibility screening for health and other benefits
CMS.gov www.cms.gov	Regulatory guidance and coverage rules for ACA and Medicare

Chapters 9–10: Trusts & S Corp Strategy

Resource	What It Provides
IRS — Small Business & Self-Employed www.irs.gov/businesses/small-businesses-self-employed	S Corp rules, reasonable compensation guidance, and tax forms
ABA — Find Legal Help www.americanbar.org/groups/legal_services/flh-home	Locate estate planning attorneys by state and specialty
ACTEC www.actec.org	Find credentialed trust and estate planning professionals
NOLO — Trusts & Estates www.nolo.com/legal-encyclopedia/trusts	Plain-language guides on wills, trusts, and estate planning

Chapter 11: Investment Red Flags

Resource	What It Provides
FINRA BrokerCheck brokercheck.finra.org	Verify broker and investment advisor registration and history
SEC Investor.gov www.investor.gov	Research investments and review SEC alerts on fraud schemes
NASAA www.nasaa.org	State securities regulator directory and investor alerts
CFP Board — Verify a CFP www.cfp.net/verify-a-cfp-professional	Confirm a financial planner's CFP credentials

PARTS III & IV — Legal Rights, Consumer Protection & Digital Safety

Chapters 12–14: Demand Letters, Evidence & Complaints

Resource	What It Provides
CFPB — File a Complaint www.consumerfinance.gov/complaint	Complaints against banks, lenders, and debt collectors
FTC — Report Fraud reportfraud.ftc.gov	Report deceptive practices, scams, and fraud to the FTC
State Attorney General Offices www.naag.org/find-my-ag	File consumer complaints at the state level
PACER.gov www.pacer.gov	Access federal civil and criminal case records
HHS OIG — Report Fraud oig.hhs.gov/fraud/report-fraud	Report Medicare and Medicaid fraud, waste, and abuse
CMS Complaint Hotline 1-800-MEDICARE (1-800-633-4227)	Report Medicare billing issues and provider concerns

Chapter 15: Scam Calls & Phone Defense

Resource	What It Provides
FTC Do Not Call Registry www.donotcall.gov	Register your number and report Do Not Call violations
FCC Consumer Complaint Center consumercomplaints.fcc.gov	Report illegal robocalls and spoofed numbers
Nomorobo www.nomorobo.com	Robocall blocking service for landlines and mobile phones
AARP Fraud Watch Network www.aarp.org/money/scams-fraud	Scam alerts, helpline (877-908-3360), and fraud reporting
IC3 — FBI Cybercrime www.ic3.gov	Report phone and internet scams to the FBI

Chapters 16–17: Smart Devices, Privacy & Digital Hygiene

Resource	What It Provides
FTC — Online Privacy Guide consumer.ftc.gov/articles/how-protect-your-privacy-online	Plain-language guidance on online privacy and device security
StaySafeOnline.org staysafeonline.org	Cybersecurity awareness guides and best practices
Have I Been Pwned haveibeenpwned.com	Check if your email was exposed in a known data breach
EFF — Privacy Tools www.eff.org	Digital rights, surveillance guidance, and privacy tools

Chapter 18: How Advertising Manipulates You

Resource	What It Provides
FTC Advertising Resources www.ftc.gov/tips-advice/business-center/advertising-and-marketing	FTC rules on deceptive advertising and endorsements
Ad Fontes Media Bias Chart adfontesmedia.com	Interactive chart rating news sources by reliability and bias
AllSides Media Bias Ratings www.allsides.com/media-bias/media-bias-ratings	Compare news source perspectives across political spectrum
MediaWise (Poynter) www.poynter.org/mediawise	Media literacy tools and fact-checking training resources

PARTS V & VI — Ethics, Stewardship & Youth Resources

Chapters 19–21: Character, Compassion & Stewardship

Resource	What It Provides
VolunteerMatch www.volunteermatch.org	Connect with local and national volunteer opportunities
Points of Light www.pointsoflight.org	Civic engagement and service leadership resources
NCOA — National Council on Aging www.ncoa.org	Programs supporting senior wellbeing and benefits access
BenefitsCheckUp (NCOA) www.benefitscheckup.org	Screen seniors for federal, state, and local benefit eligibility

Chapters 22–23: Smoking, Vaping & Substance Awareness

Resource	What It Provides
Smokefree.gov smokefree.gov	Quit smoking and vaping tools, including teen resources
CDC — Tobacco & Vaping www.cdc.gov/tobacco	Youth vaping statistics, health effects, and prevention materials
SAMHSA National Helpline 1-800-662-4357	Free, confidential substance use treatment referrals, 24/7
DEA — One Pill Can Kill www.dea.gov/onepill	Fentanyl and counterfeit pill awareness campaign for teens
Partnership to End Addiction drugfree.org	Parent guides, teen resources, and a helpline for substance concerns

Chapters 24–26: Screen Time, Diet & Teen Wellbeing

Resource	What It Provides
Common Sense Media www.commonsensemedia.org	Screen time guidance, app reviews, and digital wellness resources
AAP — Screen Time Guidelines www.healthychildren.org	Evidence-based guidelines on screen use for children and teens
CDC — Physical Activity for Teens www.cdc.gov/physicalactivity/basics/teenagers/index.htm	Recommended activity levels and teen health resources
MyPlate.gov (USDA) www.myplate.gov	Nutrition guidelines and teen eating resources
Jump$tart Coalition www.jumpstart.org	Financial literacy curriculum and resources for youth
Next Gen Personal Finance www.ngpf.org	Free personal finance education tools for high school students

GENERAL RESOURCES — Broadly Applicable Across Topics

Benefits & Eligibility Screening

Resource	What It Provides
Benefits.gov www.benefits.gov	Federal eligibility screening for 1,000+ government programs
BenefitsCheckUp (NCOA) www.benefitscheckup.org	Benefits screening tool for adults 55+
211.org — United Way www.211.org | Dial 211	Local social services, food, housing, and utility assistance

Legal Aid & Dispute Resolution

Resource	What It Provides
LawHelp.org www.lawhelp.org	Free and low-cost legal aid resources by state
ABA Free Legal Help www.americanbar.org/groups/legal_services/flh-home	Directory of legal aid programs and lawyer referral services
Better Business Bureau www.bbb.org	File complaints and research business reputations

Financial Counseling & Debt Assistance

Resource	What It Provides
NFCC — Credit Counseling www.nfcc.org	Nonprofit credit counseling and debt management referrals
CFPB Financial Tools www.consumerfinance.gov/consumer-tools	Mortgage, student loan, and debt repayment tools and guides
IRS Free File www.irs.gov/freefile	Free federal tax filing for qualifying individuals

Fact-Checking & Misinformation Detection

Resource	What It Provides
Snopes.com www.snopes.com	Fact-checking of viral claims, health rumors, and news stories
PolitiFact www.politifact.com	Nonpartisan fact-checking of political and policy claims
FactCheck.org www.factcheck.org	Nonpartisan fact-checking on political ads and speeches
AP Fact Check apnews.com/hub/ap-fact-check	Fact-checks from the Associated Press news wire

Important Note: All resources were verified as of early 2026. Websites, phone numbers, and program availability are subject to change. Always verify current information directly with the organization before taking action. This appendix is provided for informational purposes only and does not constitute legal, financial, or medical advice.

Trusted Service Providers

TRUSTED RESOURCES

Professionals Andrea Knows Personally & Recommends with Confidence

> The following professionals have been personally vetted by the author. Their integrity, competence, and commitment to the people they serve are beyond question.

1 Abba Psychotherapy Group, PLLC

Matt Miller, LPC — Houston, TX

Phone: *713-449-2225* **Web:** *abbapsych.com*

Abba Psychotherapy Group, PLLC is a Houston-based counseling practice founded by Matt Miller, LPC, specializing in therapeutic services for men and adolescent boys. The practice offers a respectful, shame-free environment where men can confront and work through trauma, abuse, addiction, anger, relationship difficulties, and identity challenges — without sacrificing their sense of self. Services are offered in four formats: individual (standard one-hour sessions), family (particularly for adolescent clients), intensive (2–3 hour sessions by special request), and group therapy organized around specific topics. The practice's three-phase therapeutic process focuses on building safety and connection, processing emotions and patterns, and achieving clarity for forward movement.

www.abbapsych.com

2 Conscious Creation Consulting LLC

Francisca Leal, M.Ed. — Houston, TX & Worldwide

In Person: *Houston, TX* **Virtual:** *Worldwide via Zoom* **Web:** *franciscaleal.com*

Conscious Creation Consulting LLC, founded by Francisca Leal, M.Ed., is an integrative coaching and wellness practice dedicated to helping individuals identify and transform limiting thought patterns so they can live empowered, inspired lives. Francisca is a Certified Master Practitioner of Neuro-Linguistic Programming (NLP), Mental and Emotional Release® (MER), and Hypnotherapy, and she holds a Master of Education in Counseling Psychology from the University of Houston. Her services include NLP-based mindset coaching, Mental and Emotional Release® therapy (for stress, anxiety, fear, depression, and phobias), hypnotherapy, and the Quit Smoking 60® technique — a clinically researched, one-session hypnosis program with a guarantee. Francisca also brings a spiritual dimension to her work, having served as a spiritual counselor and ordained minister at Unity of Houston for over a decade.

www.franciscaleal.com

3 A Better Way Chiropractic — Memorial City

Dr. Chris Schmidt — Houston, TX

Address: *8955 Katy Fwy, Suite 102, Houston, TX 77024* **Phone:** *(713) 683-6800*

A Better Way Chiropractic – Memorial City is a full-service chiropractic and wellness practice led by Dr. Chris Schmidt, dedicated to helping patients live better and feel better through expert spinal care and natural healing. The practice addresses a broad range of conditions, including back and neck pain, headaches, migraines, sciatica, shoulder and knee pain, vertigo, whiplash, auto injuries, herniated discs, scoliosis, carpal tunnel syndrome, TMJ, sports injuries, and more. The team's philosophy centers on the principle that proper spinal alignment enables the body to self-heal and perform at its best — not just for pain relief, but for overall wellness and athletic performance.

www.abetterwaychiropractic.com

Grand Pea, Inc. | *grandpeainsurance.com* | *These resources are provided for informational purposes. The author has a personal relationship with each professional listed.*

Disclaimer

This publication is intended for educational and informational purposes only and does not constitute legal, tax, or investment advice. Readers should consult qualified professionals regarding their individual circumstances.

Made in the USA
Coppell, TX
16 April 2026

75931295R00085